The
Global
Economy

THE AMERICAN ASSEMBLY was established by Dwight D. Eisenhower at Columbia University in 1950. Each year it holds at least two nonpartisan meetings that give rise to authoritative books that illuminate issues of United States policy.

An affiliate of Columbia, with offices at Barnard College, the Assembly is a national, educational institution incorporated in the state of New York.

The Assembly seeks to provide information, stimulate discussion, and evoke independent conclusions on matters of vital public interest.

CONTRIBUTORS

DAVID M. ABSHIRE, Center for Strategic and
International Studies

C. MICHAEL AHO, Council on Foreign Relations

WILLIAM E. BROCK, The Brock Group

ROBERT D. HORMATS, Goldman Sachs
International

PETER W. LUDLOW, Center for European Policy
Studies

HARALD B. MALMGREN, Malmgren, Inc.

SYLVIA OSTRY, University of Toronto

JOHN W. SEWELL, Overseas Development
Council

MICHAEL B. SMITH, SJS Advanced Strategies

RAYMOND VERNON, Harvard University

THE AMERICAN ASSEMBLY
Columbia University

The
Global Economy

*America's Role
in the Decade Ahead*

**WILLIAM E. BROCK
ROBERT D. HORMATS**
Editors

W · W · NORTON & COMPANY
New York   London

Printed in the United States of America.

The text of this book is composed in Baskerville.
Composition and manufacturing by the Haddon Craftsmen, Inc.

First Edition

Library of Congress Cataloging-in-Publication Data

The Global economy : America's role in the decade ahead / William E.
Brock, Robert D. Hormats, editors.—1st ed.
p.   cm.
Includes index.
1. Economic forecasting—United States. 2. United States—
Economic policy—1981–   3. United States—Foreign economic
relations.   4. Competition, International.   5. Twentieth century—
Forecasts.   I. Brock, William Emerson, 1930–   .   II. Hormats,
Robert D.
HC106.8.G59   1990
337.73'001—dc19   89-15972

ISBN 0-393-02805-4

ISBN 0-393-95945-7 PBK.

W. W. Norton & Company, Inc., 500 Fifth Avenue, New York, N. Y. 10110
W. W. Norton & Company Ltd., 37 Great Russell Street, London WC1B 3NU

1 2 3 4 5 6 7 8 9 0

Contents

The
Global
Economy

Preface

This is the second book published in conjunction with a series of American Assembly programs designed to examine U.S. policy options in a world that has been changing faster and more significantly than at any time since World War II. This series is based on a belief that the United States needs a long-term vision of what kind of a world it should be working to achieve by the year 2000. In particular, the shape of the world's economy needs a guiding hand, a blueprint for the decade ahead. Without such a vision we will continue to waste our energies focusing only on such short-term trade issues as baseball bats, hormones, and pasta.

The world economic system is increasingly interdependent and increasingly vulnerable; it is also increasingly multipolar and less hegemonic. What is the best global economic system to reduce that vulnerability? What should the U.S. role be, and how can we play that role given our domestic politics? Can we design and implement a system in which each country's success contributes positively to its neighbors? Is there a way for us to create a new set of global relationships in which the concept of "shared leadership" allows all of us peacefully to prosper?

The American Assembly believed that it could contribute to the development of national policy on these questions by bringing together a number of citizens who would examine the issues and come to a consensus among themselves on a vision to inspire U.S. policy. The Assembly, with the help of a steering committee (whose names are listed in an appendix), retained William Brock, former U.S. senator, secretary of labor, and U.S. special trade representative, and Robert Hormats, vice chairman of Goldman Sachs International and former assistant secretary of state and deputy trade representative, to be directors and editors of a program on managing the global economy. Under their editorial guidance, a team of authors prepared the papers in this volume to serve as background reading for the program. From April 20 to 23, 1989, a group of participants from the United States, Japan, several countries in Europe, and elsewhere in Asia met at Arden House, in Harriman, New York, to discuss the papers and to issue a report, which received wide circulation and appears as an appendix to this volume. Those background papers have been compiled in this volume, which is published as a stimulus to further thinking and discussion among informed and concerned citizens. We hope the book will serve to evoke a broad consensus about the nature of our situation and the action we should take to address it.

We are grateful to the following organizations for their support of this project:

American Express   Olin Corporation
Benton Foundation   The Overbrook Foundation
CITICORP/CITIBANK   Rockefeller Family &
The Ford Foundation   Associates
The Ford Motor Company   Volvo
General Electric Foundation   Xerox Foundation
The German Marshall Fund
of the U.S.

The opinions expressed in this volume are those of the individual authors and not necessarily of the sponsors or The American Assembly, which takes no position on subjects it presents for public discussion.

Daniel A. Sharp
President
The American Assembly

Introduction

WILLIAM E. BROCK
AND
ROBERT D. HORMATS

Writing a book on managing the global economy in less than a couple of hundred pages is like trying to sum up the Olympic Games with a single snap of your 35-mm camera. At least in this case we have, in the hands of several very tal-

WILLIAM E. BROCK is president of The Brock Group, a Washington consulting firm specializing in international trade, investment, labor-management relations, and human resource issues. Beginning in 1962, Senator Brock served four terms in the U.S. Congress, elected as the first Republican in over forty years to represent Tennessee's Third District. In 1970 he was elected to the United States Senate, where he served on the Finance, Banking, and Government Operations committees. From 1977 to 1981, Senator Brock was nominated by the Republican party to serve as their national chair. Senator Brock was appointed United States trade representative in 1981, where he served as President Reagan's chief trade advisor and negotiator until 1985. He was named secretary of labor in 1985, a position he held until 1987.

ROBERT D. HORMATS is vice chair of Goldman Sachs International, with responsibility for development and execution of the

ented authors, more than one camera. But we are sure all
would admit we can at best only begin a very long, complex,
and important conversation.

For those of us in the United States, the glory days of un-
challenged economic superiority have been replaced by years
of monumental economic challenges on our own turf by Japan,
the increasingly dynamic economies of Asia (the new tigers),
as well as the resurgent nations of Europe.

Yes, we are better and stronger than we were a few years
ago. Yes, we are still enjoying the longest economic recovery
in U.S. postwar history. And yes, our companies in the main
have stripped down many nonessential overhead burdens,
focused on customers and new markets, and improved productivity. These, coupled with a more realistically priced dollar, mean that at the moment we are more competitive than we
were only a few years ago. Perhaps of greater long-term consequence, most Americans now know future progress must be
earned on a competitive international field, not merely accepted as a birthright.

Yet America is only beginning to adjust to this reality. There
is a dangerous tendency to believe that our economy is so
inherently strong that it will thrive no matter what policies are
applied to it, and a similarly dangerous tendency to blame

---

firm's business in Western Europe and Canada. Mr. Hormats has a
long career of government service in the executive branch, beginning
in 1969, when he was staff member for international economic affairs
with the National Security Council, a post he held until 1973. After a
year as guest scholar at the Brookings Institution, on a fellowship
from the Council on Foreign Relations, Mr. Hormats returned to the
NSC as senior staff member for international economic affairs. From
1977 to 1979 he served as deputy assistant secretary of state for economic and business affairs, and from 1979 to 1981 as deputy U.S.
trade representative, with the rank of ambassador. In 1981 and 1982,
prior to joining Goldman Sachs, Mr. Hormats was assistant secretary
of state for economic and business affairs. His publications include
several books on international monetary and financial issues and articles in *Foreign Affairs,* the *New York Times,* the *Washington Post, American
Banker,* and the *Financial Times* of London.

many of our problems on the trade practices or competitive strategy of other nations—a notion that can too easily distract us from the formidable task we face at home. At home, savings and loans crises compete for headlines with the monotonous alliteration of deficits, debts, and dollar disturbances. After spending more in total, and per child, on education of our young than any other nation, the result is a miserable performance in math, science, and reasoning skills, only slightly ahead of Hungary, but behind every other major competitor. After spending $600,000 per farmer in farm support, we have fewer farms and a smaller share of the world agricultural market. After reducing tax rates to their lowest level in decades, our savings rate remains the lowest in the industrial world, our investment per worker half that of Japan.

Globally, the world economy, as it exists today, might be virtually unrecognizable to many who sought to frame and shape its institutions in the 1940s; yet the basic international instruments they evolved remain. The specialized agencies of trade and finance still act in defense of multilateral principles, though the task may very well exceed their grasp, at least as presently formulated.

The General Agreement on Tariffs and Trade (GATT) is a case in point. Formed when it became obvious that the much more comprehensive proposed ITO (International Trade Organization) was unachievable, it nonetheless has provided yeoman service to the world in facilitating expansion of trade in goods. Here a steady stream of officials has assembled in successive rounds of negotiations to lower tariffs, settle seemingly intractable disputes, and reduce unavoidable tensions. As a result, it has helped growth in world trade to provide a major engine of progress for the world, and for most nations individually.

Yet as the tide of high tariffs receded, it left exposed a host of nontariff barriers, subsidies, and discriminatory regulatory practices. Additionally, early on efforts to involve (or compromise with, or mollify) developing countries resulted in giving them a general exception to the rules and disciplines of the

GATT. In letting developing nations out from many obligations to abide by GATT discipline we may have made them temporarily happy, but we did them no favor. The rules are there because they benefit all parties, not just the well-to-do. More importantly, these well-intended negotiations left the GATT with a potentially fatal wound. Many of those nations, then impoverished, are now very tough and adept competitors. Yet we have given them the right of self-designation as "developing," and therefore they are allowed special and differential treatment (i.e., rules can be violated and trading partners abused with impunity). That cannot continue without undermining the contractual system itself.

More broadly, as the growth of service industries became the most significant factor in world employment growth, the GATT only belatedly considered its obvious responsibilities in this area. Further, informatics, satellites, and the free flow of capital and ideas made intellectual property, patents, trademarks, and copyrights areas of increasing importance—and areas in which there were increasing abuses. The world had created WIPO (the World Intellectual Property Organization), but it gave it no tools with which to act. Research and development is our source of hope for long-term improvement in the well-being, health, and employment of the world's peoples. Its encouragement, through protection of intellectual property, is of crucial importance to continued progress of the world and its trading system. In the face of this fact, we see WIPO, the only presently relevant organization, as a shell, without will or authority. This in turn has left the GATT exposed to new and debilitating charges of inadequate coverage and competitiveness.

Fortunately, the current round of trade negotiations has on its agenda services and intellectual property. Much will depend on the way these issues are resolved in the current round of the GATT negotiations. All of this is to say the world economy has developed much faster than the trade organization that serves to nurture and sustain trade within a climate that is both fair and predictable.

In similar fashion, both the World Bank, which was created to provide financial support to postwar reconstruction and major projects in the developing world, and the International Monetary Fund (IMF), which was to provide temporary funding for short-term balance-of-payments difficulties, find that the world is increasingly looking to them for solutions to the long-term debt problem that so beleaguers nations in Latin America and around the globe. Further, massive capital movements, unanticipated at the creation of the Bretton Woods institutions, play havoc with economies and markets; yet there is little these institutions can do, or perhaps, should do, to stabilize them. And currency volatility has, until recently, posed great uncertainty for trade and investment—again raising issues that defy easy institutional answers.

In truth we are asking both financial and trade organizations to consider new issues and take on much larger responsibilities than were ever envisioned.

The global community is facing dramatic change. The new technologies, the Uruguay Round, the United States–Canada Free Trade Agreement, Europe 1992, the massive trade imbalance that exists between Japan and the United States, economic as well as political ferment in the Communist world, and Third World debt are major issues that are profoundly altering the way the United States operates within the international community.

The world has undergone a radical transformation since 1945. It is so interdependent and complex that the United States can no longer create a policy to address one major economic issue without considering the effect that it will have on other issues, or other nations, or even on the global economic system as a whole. Nor can economic issues be considered in isolation from politics. They are critical components of America's overall set of political and security relationships in the world. Indeed an America, which by its internal and international policies loses its dynamism, is also likely to see its political and alliance leadership weakened. Short-sighted policies can be suicidal in such an interdependent world.

This then is a difficult context, within which our authors

must employ their talents for analysis, foresight, and policy selection.

Ray Vernon starts us in the right direction with what he describes as a synoptic view of the last forty years. Ray rightly notes the enormous importance of the postwar consensus among U.S. leaders and the consequence of that consensus in terms of a coherent and remarkably farsighted U.S. postwar policy. Stemming from the shared years of the twenties, the crash, the Great Depression, and the Second World War, these men and women evolved a set of intrinsic values rooted in their common personal experience.

Slowly at first, more rapidly of late, new forces have shaken the consensus. Insufficiently mentioned, but to us of fundamental importance, was the declining capacity of governments to exercise control over events. The result: frustration, and a temptation to intervene through protectionism and subsidy.

Economic interdependence has created an obvious need for governmental acts of cooperation with other nations, acts that have been difficult at best for the U.S. in the face of divided authority and divided views in our nation's capital.

Management and labor, government and business, all of us face a tumultuous time of great pressure on individuals and institutions. Governmental efforts to ease the transition by new and more appropriate tax, education, training, and related adjustment efforts will be imperative. Ill-conceived initiatives to halt the change itself, on the other hand, could be suicidal.

Europe faces a similarly daunting task. There twelve nations have embarked upon what may be the most important political act of this century. They have committed to unify their economies into a single market. Until passage of the Single Europe Act, thirty years of rhetoric without adequate action had bred skepticism. Today Europe truly seems embarked upon a process that has huge public support and its own growing momentum. Peter Ludlow takes us step-by-step through the process and to the inevitable conclusion of not just a unified market, but a remarkably different geopolitical world.

If our hope is to exercise some rational coordination and

cooperation, if not management, in the global economy, it is hard to conceive of a more important international event than the unification of Europe and the potential consequence of that act for U.S. policy, for a newly evolved U.S.–European relationship, and for East-West relations.

On the next page of our Mercator projection of the globe is Japan, wrapped in all of its new-found muscle. Michael Smith in chapter 3 is quick to point out that with all our focus and fascination with Europe, nothing is "more pressing or seemingly more intractable than the American relationship with Japan." He is right of course. The need for us to simultaneously consider and deal with this fact is symptomatic of the global straddle of the United States and the imperative of keeping our attention focused on virtually all areas simultaneously.

Mike proceeds to suggest a number of concrete steps that can help weave these two nations into an economic relationship that is mutually beneficial. Avoiding the temptation for a simple bilateral free trade agreement between us, which he discounts, Mike then suggests instead the development of a Pacific Rim economic arrangement which would undertake a constant liberalization of trade in excess of the pace we can anticipate for the GATT contracting parties.

Like the GATT, the global economy is vulnerable to unanticipated and uncontrollable forces, embodied in the awesome capabilities of new technologies. Hal Malmgren explores this issue in our fourth chapter. In the information revolution, new materials, new transportation, new manufacturing techniques, new technologies, and new biotechnology all appear in such rapid succession. This pace of change has shaken the very foundation of most of society's institutions, public and private.

Our well-being will be increasingly dependent upon our ability and our willingness to adapt to this pace. It is also imperative that the developing nations be able to take advantage of technological changes. If the developing world cannot, the difference between the haves and have-nots will constrain the future growth of the U.S. and the global economy.

This leads us naturally into John Sewell's discussion of our relationship with the developing world. John notes the enormous divergence between the several nations generally categorized as the "Third World." Disaggregating them into at least three categories, if not more, he notes the different approaches U.S. policy must pursue in dealing with the particular interests and problems of each of these groups of nations. Diverse as they are, we must clearly understand the crucial consequence their collective well-being can have for the United States and the Western world.

Noting the urgency of resource, growth, and debt problems, John proposes a common effort to increase transfers from surplus countries, to open developed country markets, to maximize trade and growth, and to more effectively use international agencies. He notes the essential component of putting our own economic house in order, in both monetary and fiscal terms—a theme that recurs throughout the book.

We left it to Michael Aho and Sylvia Ostry to take on the question posed by huge regional trading blocs and their presence within a multilateral system. Their defense of the multilateral system is articulate and effective. They note with concern the changing style and content of U.S. trade policies, particularly our increasing willingness to exercise the political leverage that goes with economic power.

Mike and Sylvia lead us very carefully back to the inescapable conclusion that, in the final analysis, a multilateral system is the only one that is sustainable and of sufficiently universal application to be worthy of an investment of real consequence on our part.

Finally, David Abshire writes the prospective. David has a wonderful talent to weave together all the significant geopolitical, economic, social, and security elements into a coherent whole. He builds upon what has gone before—the changes in the system, the multiple facets of power and the various combinations thereof, the urgency of achieving domestic economic reform, and restoration of our international competitiveness. He takes time to discuss the *process* by which leadership is achieved within the United States, draws our attention again to the multilateral institutions, and finally considers the summit and the summit nations.

David leaves us with a clear sense of the magnitude of the difficulties in front of us, and yet with a welcome sense of our capacity to meet and overcome those challenges as a free people. The tools, after all, are ours to use, if we will. It is an appropriate note on which to terminate this first stage of our conversation.

1

Same Planet, Different Worlds

RAYMOND VERNON

Looking back on 1950 with the perspective of four decades, it is easy to identify some of the breathtaking changes that have altered the character of U.S. society and modified the country's relationship to the rest of the world. Less obvious but no less important have been some of the persistent characteristics and enduring values that the United States and other countries have carried unchanged into the new era. Propelled by technological, economic, and political changes, yet restrained at the same time by longstanding values and institutions, the United States is being challenged to develop new policies that will help it respond to the changed international environment in which it is obliged to operate.

RAYMOND VERNON is Clarence Dillon Professor of International Affairs Emeritus at Harvard University, where he has served in various capacities since 1959. In addition to his distinguished career at Harvard, he has also held several positions at the Securities and Exchange Commission and at the U.S. Department of State. Dr. Vernon has published numerous books and articles on the international economy, including, most recently, *Beyond Globalism: Remaking American Foreign Economic Policy* (coauthored with Debora L. Spar).

A Synoptic View, 1950 and 1990

The Scene in 1950

With the advantage of forty years of hindsight, it is apparent that the early 1950s represented an extraordinary period in American history.

One unusual characteristic of the period was the extent to which American leaders from all sectors of the American economy shared a view of the role that the United States should play in the international economy. During the turbulent decades of the 1930s and 1940s, national leaders from business, labor, agriculture, and politics faced repeated threats and crises from the international environment, from a deep depression to a global war. Their shared experiences in meeting these crises had helped to produce some shared values, including a widespread agreement on the desirability of an open international economy under U.S. leadership.

These shared values were not so inclusive as to put an end to controversy over the international policies of the country or to suppress the operation of the country's system of checks and balances. A Democratic administration, for instance, confronted with widespread opposition from the business community, was obliged in 1950 to abandon a project for a proposed international trade organization, a project on which bureaucrats had labored for over half a decade. Still, the degree of consensus in the national leadership on such issues was quite extraordinary in a national political system whose normal method of decision making was one of struggle among competing interests. That pervasive consensus made it possible for the United States to conduct the military occupation of Germany and Japan with a degree of magnanimity unmatched in modern history. It allowed American leaders to introduce and execute the idea of a special program of aid for Greece and Turkey, a Marshall Plan for Europe, and a so-called Point Four program of technical assistance for developing countries.

The strength of the consensus among U.S. leaders was increased by a universal view of the technological dominance of the U.S. economy. Any sense among Americans of technological inferiority such as had existed in many quarters after World War I was gone, replaced by a feeling of unassailable superiority in the technological domain.

The facts provided ample support for the feeling of superiority. By the 1940s and 1950s, the United States was providing a majority of the world's Nobel laureates in the sciences and a majority of the world's notable inventions. Stimulated by the extraordinary demands of a decade of war and of postwar reconstruction, the United States had managed to extend its technological lead over potential European competitors to unprecedented proportions; for perhaps the first time in the modern industrial era, Americans seemed to be holding the lead in practically every major industrial field, including even those branches of industry that had been the traditional domain of European producers, such as chemicals, pharmaceuticals, and machine tools.

The sheer economic dominance of the United States in the global economy in 1950 added to the sense of invulnerability that most Americans shared. Per capita income in the United States was substantially higher than that of every European country, and six or eight times higher than that of Japan. The U.S. balance of payments recorded large current account surpluses in spite of a heavy outflow of foreign aid; indeed, in 1950 the United States was the only large industrialized country that was free of balance-of-payment problems and related import restriction. The U.S. economy, with nearly 40 percent of the output of the industrialized world and over half of its monetary gold, seemed economically impregnable at the time.

The political and military alliances of the United States in 1950 added to the sense of unity, self-assurance, and leadership that characterized the U.S. role in 1950. The policy of containment of the Soviet bloc provided a relatively unambiguous doctrine for dealing with a recognized enemy. Military alliances in Europe and the South Pacific gave U.S. forces secure forward bases in various parts of the world, distant from the home territory. All these factors made it easy for the United States to take the lead against the Communist countries in blocking the conquest of South Korea and in restricting the bloc's access to military technology.

To be sure, the sense of invulnerability among Americans was not to endure for very long. The USSR's rapidly expanding nuclear capabilities would soon excite deep unease among Americans, intensified by the launching of the Sputnik a few years later. For a decade or so thereafter, Americans would labor to close a real or fancied missile gap and would try to create a credible system of civil defense. But as of 1950 the real long-term threat was seen to be directed at countries in Europe, Asia, and Latin America, rather than at the United States itself.

The Scene in 1990

The unusual degree of consensus prevalent in 1950 could not be expected to endure for long in a system that encouraged policy making through struggle. Long before 1990, the system of checks and balances on which the U.S. government is fundamentally based had fully reasserted itself, reflecting a structure that one eminent political scientist described as "the strangest system on earth." The courts had acquired substantial new powers to restrain or command the executive. The Congress had greatly expanded its committee structures, its professional staffs, and its legal prerogatives to monitor and modify the performance of the executive branch. Newspapers had developed a practice of investigative reporting reminiscent of the Lincoln Steffens era before World War I. And interest group organizations multiplied their presence in Washington many times over in order to exploit their greatly enlarged access to the decision-making process.

American perceptions of the technological capabilities of the U.S. economy also had greatly changed. The United States was still far ahead of other countries in national expenditures on research and development; but a high proportion of that research was devoted to military objectives, and there were widespread misgivings that those expenditures might be hampering achievements in nonmilitary programs. U.S. graduate programs in science and engineering were unmatched in size and richness, but half the graduates and a considerable proportion of the faculty in these programs were non-American. U.S.–based firms still held the technological lead over a larger part of the world's industrial frontiers than the firms of any other country, including a commanding position in aeronautics, telecommunications, and the exotic areas of biotechnology; but they had surrendered the lead or were being severely challenged in many branches of industry, notably in consumer electronics, machine tools, automobiles, and steel processing.

The four decades also had seen a remarkable change in the relative incomes of Americans. American incomes were of course far higher in 1990 than in 1950, both in real and in nominal terms. But by 1990 the living standards of the populations of Germany, Japan, Switzerland, and Sweden were approaching those of the United States. The catch-up in living standards was based on a growth of productivity in each of these countries that exceeded that of the United States for much of the period. Related to that record was the fact that U.S. savings rates in 1990 were among the lowest in the industrialized world.

Just as striking was the changed position of the United States in the international economy. Although the United States continued to hold a dominant place in world trade and investment, its relative position was substantially reduced. U.S. output had accounted for about 38 percent of world output in 1950, but it was down to about 27 percent in 1990. U.S. merchandise exports, which had amounted to about 20 percent of world exports in the early 1950s, had slipped to about 10 percent by 1990. In 1950 the foreign direct investments of U.S.–based firms were greater than the foreign direct investments of firms based in all other countries combined; by 1990, however, firms based in Europe and Japan had built up their overseas investments to totals that nearly tripled the U.S. totals.

The most striking change in the relative position of the U.S. economy during these decades was in its relation to Japan.

During the four decades from 1950 to 1990, the increases in
Japan's productivity and gross national product were more
rapid and more sustained than those of any other industrialized country. Starting from scratch in 1950, Japanese exports
in 1990 came to about 10 percent of world exports, matching
the U.S. total. Japanese banks were carving out large niches in
international money markets; indeed, seven of the world's ten
largest banks were based in Japan, and 40 percent of the total
assets of the world's 100 largest banks was accounted for by
the Japanese. And Japanese industry was developing a major
stake abroad in the form of branches and subsidiaries, with
particularly heavy investment concentrations in North America and Southeast Asia. By 1990 the foreign direct investments
of Japanese firms were approaching $50 billion; that total was
still only a fraction of the total for U.S. firms, but it was growing much faster.

Accompanying the changes in the relative position of the
U.S. economy was a marked change in its balance of payments.
The large positive current account balances and heavy capital
outflows that had typified the 1950s were reversed; by 1990
the United States was importing capital in large amounts to
finance its government debt and industrial investment, while
recording large negative balances on current account. There
was fear in some quarters that a continuation of that trend over
a number of additional years could generate such high claims
on the U.S. economy in the form of dividends and debt servic-
ing as to arrest the country's economic growth.

Some of the changes that produced the reversal in the U.S.
current account between 1950 and 1990 were particularly disturbing to U.S. policy makers. One of these was the sharp reversal in the U.S. national position with regard to oil. From a
state of self-sufficiency in 1950, the U.S. economy by 1990 was
importing nearly half of its petroleum needs. That shift was
producing anxieties that rivaled those created by the decline in
U.S. technological dominance.

During those four decades, despite changes in the relative
position of the U.S. economy, some of the country's funda-

mental assumptions regarding its national security interests remained essentially unchanged. Americans still accepted the idea that the United States must maintain a military establishment second to none. And they still took it for granted that U.S. security interests were global rather than regional, justifying such measures as patrolling Persian Gulf waters, supporting Afghan rebels, and bombing Libya. On the other hand, U.S. control over its forward bases in various parts of the world had become considerably weaker, as various allies limited U.S. access to such bases. Moreover, the cost of maintaining U.S. leadership in the North Atlantic Treaty Organization (NATO) was being questioned with increasing frequency.

In other respects, too, the American security position was undergoing a considerable shift. The earlier preoccupation with the Soviet threat was giving way to a realization that the security problems of the future could come from different directions. Americans seemed eager to accept the overtures of President Mikhail Gorbachev as a harbinger of better relations with the USSR. If there were enemies still to be reckoned with, they appeared to be a succession of lesser leaders found in countries such as Syria, Cuba, Iran, Nicaragua, and Libya.

Behind these remarkable changes in the position of the U.S. economy and the attitudes of the American people lay some strong forces—political, technological, and economic.

Forces of Change, 1950 to 1990

Changing Politics

The years from 1950 to 1990 saw some profound changes in the domestic politics of the United States. Some of these developments pushed U.S. politics into new and previously untrod territory. But many represented a return to fundamental characteristics of the country's political system, a resumption and intensification of patterns shaped by the constitutional structure of checks and balances and by the deep-seated American preference to limit the power and influence of the federal government.

It is worth recalling that the constitutional structure reflected a deliberate decision of the Founding Fathers to avoid a highly centralized national government, and by avoiding a centralized government, to reduce the risk that some person or party or region of the country might be able to shape the policies of the United States to suit its interests, without regard for the conflicting interests of others. An inescapable corollary of that decision was that federal policies would be shaped through a process of continuous struggle, a process that could at times produce results that appeared contradictory and inconsistent.

Within a decade or two after the dangers of depression and war had been overcome, these basic characteristics of U.S. politics began to reassert themselves. With the resumption of politics as usual, the American consensus behind the movement toward open international markets became more qualified. As long as the issue of open markets arose in the form of support for a general principle, unattached to any specific product or service, both political parties continued to lend their support, repeatedly giving broad authority to the president to negotiate with other countries for the reduction of existing trade barriers. But over time the Democrats manifested mounting concern for the interests of workers in individual industries that were being adversely affected by the increased volume of imports; increasingly they threw their weight in support of provisions that would allow an imperiled group to get special relief from the effects of the trend toward more open markets.

Other developments contributed to bringing the unusual period of consensus to a close. During most of the forty years between 1950 and 1990, at least one of the two houses of Congress would be controlled by the opposition party. The Vietnam War and the Watergate episode accentuated the importance of checks and balances and intensified the use of struggle as the normal process of U.S. decision making. Checks and balances among the branches of the federal government grew more pervasive. The Congress, for instance, developed an array of so-called congressional vetoes, and it greatly enlarged the corps of professionals in the congressional committees on Capitol Hill who could be used to do battle with the executive agencies. Concurrently, the federal courts acquired new powers through statute or through precedent, which gave them a basis for intervening more directly in the administrative activities of the executive. The public at large was also equipped with added powers, in the form of "freedom of information laws" and "sunshine laws," enlarging public access to the processes and records of the federal agencies. A striking increase occurred in the volume of litigation, legislative hearings, and administrative procedures associated with the processes of the federal government. These developments, in turn, reduced even further the capacity of the government to avoid measures that on the surface appeared inconsistent or contradictory in direction and purpose.

One policy that the federal government could pursue with a certain measure of consistency in the political climate of the 1980s was the policy of shrinking back the regulatory powers of government over the economic life of the country. Throughout most of the world, including the Communist countries, the governmental role was cut back, as official controls were loosened and the role of state owned enterprises reduced.

One can only speculate as to the causes of the global trend toward curtailing the role of the state in economic affairs. One hypothesis is that over most of the forty-year period, economists and planners were gradually realizing some of the limitations in the ability of governments to manage economic policies that would produce desired results. The hope of Europe's Social Democrats in the 1960s to manage their economies by controlling key industries—the so-called commanding heights of the economy—produced deeply disappointing results. The disconcerting international disturbances of the 1970s shook the confidence of economists and planners even further, as they tried unsuccessfully to cope with wild increases in the price of oil. The huge debt crises of the early 1980s, affecting especially countries in Latin America and Africa, were also thought to have weakened the confidence of government officials in their ability to manage their economies.

By 1990 some pressures appeared to be developing to return governments to a more active role. Worries over the environment, including nuclear and chemical waste and the impairment of the ozone, were mounting. The illegal movement of people from poor countries into Europe and North America was stirring increasing concern. Huge flows of capital across international borders were raising fears among Americans and others that their ability to control their own economies might be draining away. The roller coaster behavior of the prices of some key commodities such as oil and of some key currencies such as the U.S. dollar was also stirring misgivings. Whether these developments presaged a return to a more activist role for governments in international economic relations was not yet clear.

Changing Technology

Of the various factors that transformed the U.S. relationship to the international economic environment between 1950 and 1990, technological innovation heads the list. Particularly important has been a group of innovations that drastically reduced the cost and increased the mobility of capital, people, and information across national borders.

In communication, the development of extraterrestrial satellites, optic fibers, computerized switching devices, and telex and fax machines dramatically reduced the inescapable uncertainties, the delays, and the substantial costs that were a feature of transoceanic services. By 1990 the prices of international communication, when measured in real terms, were about one-twentieth those of 1950.

Meanwhile, the prices for long-distance travel and shipping in real terms fell to one-third or one-quarter of their levels in 1950. The containerization of freight and commercial air cargo, both unknown before 1950, increased the reliability and lowered the cost of transporting foreign goods to processors, assemblers, and wholesalers. Those developments in turn revolutionized the logistical patterns of industry, allowing enterprises to use foreign sources of supply as an integral part of their procurement networks. The growth and spread of scheduled commercial air routes turned long-distance travel from a rare experience reserved for diplomats, executives, and princes into a facility routinely available for tourists, students, sales representatives, and technicians.

Some technological developments during the four decades from 1950 to 1990, however, had a special significance for the position of the United States. Recall that the period began with the United States in a position of unprecedented technological dominance, built up during the war years and the immediate postwar period. That dominance, as various studies confirm, was due in considerable part to the fact that U.S. business representatives and U.S. technicians were operating in a national market environment that was distinctive in various ways. The U.S. national market was the largest in size anywhere in the world; its people enjoyed the world's highest per capita incomes; and its producers bore hourly labor costs that were among the world's highest, while benefiting from capital and raw materials costs that were among the world's lowest. In that distinctive environment, the innovations of U.S. enterprises tended to cluster in two areas: satisfying the new wants generated by the world's highest incomes, such as television sets and freezers; and reducing the relative use of high-cost labor in favor of low-cost capital, such as forklift trucks, earth-moving equipment, and dishwashing machines.

In the first two decades following World War II, innovations of this sort found a ready market in the rest of the world, as incomes and labor costs rose toward U.S. levels and as capital became increasingly available in foreign markets. By the 1970s, however, two things grew evident: first, that enterprises in other countries were mastering and improving on the innovations that the Americans had piled up in earlier decades; and second, that foreign enterprises were acquiring or reestablishing a capacity to innovate along lines not very different from those of U.S. producers.

The innovations that emerged from Europeans and the Japanese firms eventually proved more appropriate to their home markets than the American prototypes had been. The Europeans, for instance, quickly learned to downsize refrigerators and automobiles in order to serve buyers with income levels that were somewhat lower than those prevailing in the United States; and the Japanese learned to miniaturize household appliances and electronic devices in order to conserve on the scarcest of Japan's resources, namely, living space.

The European and Japanese innovations were given a further boost by the vast increases in oil prices in the 1970s and by the increasing emphasis on avoiding environmental degradation. Responding to their relative lack of energy and other raw materials, the Europeans and the Japanese had characteristically concentrated on innovations that economized on such inputs. Suddenly, in the 1970s, products and processes capable of conserving on energy and other raw materials provided a new competitive edge in world markets.

By 1990, however, there were signs that technology was beginning to exert a new set of influences on the international competitiveness of the United States and other countries, influences that seemed far more complex than in 1950 or 1970.

For one thing, most large enterprises in the world, wherever they were located, had a much greater capacity for scanning distant places in order to learn about their potentials as markets. As a consequence, one could not assume quite so readily that firms headquartered in any given country would draw their principal stimulus for innovations primarily out of the conditions in the home market. At times, distant markets were beginning to provide the stimulus, as Japanese firms were able to demonstrate by their introduction of civilian-band radios in the United States. The technological advantages that U.S. firms had once possessed arising out of their location in the United States were no longer so strong. Some vestiges of those advantages still remained, to be sure, especially in those industries that served military needs. But there was no prospect that U.S. firms could retain the extraordinary technological lead that they had enjoyed in 1950.

Another major development was a sharp increase in the flexibility of manufacturing facilities, a development based on the increased use of the computer in design and manufacture. The introduction of those new processes meant that production facilities in many industries tended to be more flexible and less fully dedicated to specified products. This tendency, in turn, meant that the analysis required for identifying least-cost production sites was not nearly as obvious as it had once been and that the results of any such analysis were not nearly as conclusive. For instance, countries with large pools of unskilled labor were discovering that some labor-intensive processes in the semiconductor industry were being performed by new computer directed processes operating in countries with higher labor costs. Particularly threatening to developing countries was the prospect that the cutting and sewing of clothing would soon be done by such processes.

New technological developments were threatening the relative positions of developing countries in other ways as well. One of these was the long-term trend toward conservation in the use of raw materials, including a trend away from the use of metals toward the use of plastics and ceramics. Another was the increased efficiency in the use of energy, which appeared to be persisting in spite of relatively low prices for petroleum. Finally, the developing countries were facing the bleak prospect that their students and workers might not have the opportunities to master computer technology sufficient to keep up with the richer countries, and that the gap in productivity and income might accordingly widen.

Changing Enterprise Structures

As the facilities for international communication and travel continued to improve during the four decades from 1950 to 1990, and as large enterprises in every country found it easier to scan remote areas for business opportunities, the reasons for establishing subsidiaries in foreign countries increased substantially. At the same time, the costs of controlling and directing such subsidiaries after they were established went down. As a result, large enterprises headquartered in the United States, Europe, and Japan rapidly began to build up networks of subsidiaries outside their home territories. U.S. firms had led the movement in the 1950s and 1960s, so that multinational enterprises were widely regarded at first as a peculiarly American development, an aspect of the existence of an American hegemony over the non-Communist world. In the 1970s and 1980s, however, it became apparent that the trend was universal, involving not only most large firms in Europe and Japan, but even a number of large firms in developing countries such as India and Brazil as well as some large firms headquartered in China and the USSR.

By 1990 it was clear that the movement toward the multinationalization of enterprises was based on powerful factors that would not easily be reversed. After a few years of uncertainty in the early 1980s, U.S.–based multinational enterprises resumed their overseas growth, so that by 1990 their foreign subsidiaries and branches had about 7 million employees and represented over $250 billion in investment. Meanwhile, European and Japanese firms were building up their stake as well; in the United States alone, their subsidiaries accounted for about 3 million employees, while their total investments outside their respective home countries amounted to over $500 billion, more than twice the U.S. total.

The strength of the multinationalization trend was exhibited in more subtle ways as well. In 1950 innovating multinational firms had almost universally followed the practice of producing and introducing their innovations first of all in their home markets, to be followed eventually by production and sale through their subsidiaries in foreign markets. By 1990, however, firms were commonly producing and introducing their innovations without delay in foreign markets.

Moreover, by 1990 there were strong signs that some

smaller firms were finding it advantageous to develop a multi-national network, especially firms that held dominant technological positions in niches of the market.

The increasing ease with which enterprises could overcome the frictions created by distance led not only to the rapid growth of multinational enterprises but also to a new wave of alliances that linked potential competitors. These alliances took various forms. AT&T, for instance, acquired minority equity interests in a number of European firms engaged in electronics and communications. Each of the principal U.S. automobile manufacturers developed joint ventures with Japanese firms engaged in the manufacture of cars and trucks. Both Boeing and McDonnell-Douglas developed consortia with European and Japanese firms to finance, produce, and market their aircraft.

As a rule, several motives existed for these consortia. Spreading financial risk, opening up markets that otherwise would be closed, and pooling complementary technological skills were among factors encouraging the growth of consortia. In most of those cases, especially where each of the parties continued to operate a large part of its business independently of the other, one could be reasonably sure that mergers were not in the offing and that the alliances would be only temporary. That prospect was particularly likely for firms engaged in lines that governments saw as vital to national security, such as aircraft and telecommunications; in such cases, governments usually resisted any mergers that overtly placed national firms under the control of foreigners. Still, the alliances represented another illustration of the increasing prominence in the 1990s of institutional links in the economic relations between countries.

One consequence of the increase in such links was especially important. Forty years earlier, the international flow of technology, capital, and goods had been mainly the result of arm's length transactions across international borders between independent parties. By 1990, however, a considerable part of these flows represented transfers between units of a single multinational enterprise or between the members of a consortium.

No precise data exist on the importance of these internal transfers in relation to total international transactions. A hint of their relative importance, however, can be seen in the fact that the exports of U.S.–based firms to their foreign subsidiaries amounted to about 30 percent of total U.S. merchandise exports; and the exports of Japanese-based firms to their foreign subsidiaries represented about the same proportion of total Japanese exports. It is also likely that internal transfers figured more prominently in the movement of technology and high-tech products than in bulk commodities, adding to the importance of such transactions.

Changing Security Issues

In 1950 the prevailing U.S. view of its security problems was comparatively simple: the Communist bloc was the enemy, and the appropriate policy was one of containment. The principal military means for containment were alliances such as NATO, backed up ultimately by the power of nuclear weapons.

In that setting, U.S. policy makers sought to deny goods and technology to the Communist bloc that might contribute to its war-making potential and to avoid measures that might contribute to the economic growth of those countries. Accordingly, the U.S. government subjected transactions with the enemy to very tight controls and tried to persuade other countries to join in such efforts.

On the other hand, the economic policies of the United States in 1950 responded to other factors besides security. Few distinctions were made, for instance, between the economic treatment accorded to allies such as other NATO members and the treatment accorded to "nonaligned" countries such as India and Brazil. Even the bilateral foreign aid programs of the United States that gained prominence in the 1960s exhibited only loose ties to the country's military objectives.

In the decades following 1950, the idea that transactions with the Communist bloc should be strictly controlled lost ground from time to time, then gained in strength again under the impact of such events as the Berlin blockade, the Cuban missile crisis, and the Vietnam War. But doubts about the feasibility and even the relevance of the containment concept persisted. By 1990 the containment concept had lost a little ground in American public opinion, while the disposition grew to look cautiously for ways to build confidence and mitigate tensions between Communist and non-Communist countries.

Behind that shift were a number of different factors. Not the least of these was the gradual realization among politicians and in the public that nuclear weapons were like none other: although these weapons were a mortal threat, they were a threat that could not be used to swing the military balance in favor of one of the superpowers. The difficult idea that mutually assured destruction might bolster the chances for peace gradually took hold. That hard-won lesson was raised in question by President Ronald Reagan's Strategic Defense Initiative, a fact that explains the level of passion with which the Reagan initiative was debated. But by 1990 those who hoped to be able to find a new basis for peace by inventing defenses against nuclear weapons seemed to be acknowledging that a technological means for doing so was not at hand. That realization helped to create a favorable climate in the latter 1980s for the Gorbachev proposals to reduce the levels of tension between East and West.

Other factors also contributed to the change in the political climate. One was the gradual recognition in the United States of the limited effectiveness of restrictions on the flow of technology in restraining the Soviet war-making potential. Another was the enormous cost of defense, a burden that limited increases in expenditures on social programs in the United States and Europe and that appeared to be placing a heavy strain on the Soviet economy as well.

Nevertheless, the security problems of the United States in 1990 still seemed formidable. For one thing, the process of reducing tensions between the two superpowers had only begun, with major uncertainties whether the process would be followed to a satisfactory conclusion. Unless or until the United States changed its fundamental defense policies, it would be faced with the difficult problem of maintaining its military capabilities and holding together its alliances sufficiently to deal with an abrupt reversal in the trend toward lower tensions.

Meanwhile, the U.S. capacity to maintain its military capabilities was being threatened not only by budgetary constraints but by other factors as well. Two factors in particular were concerning U.S. policy makers: the increase in the capabilities of "smart" weapons, capable of pinpointing military installations; and the decline in the U.S. hold on its forward bases, including naval facilities in the Philippines, Spain, and Greece as well as U.S. rights to overfly many countries.

Another factor that was changing U.S. perceptions as to the nature of its security problems in 1990 was the increasing capacity of small states and of nonstate groups to apply destructive force. That threat had been recognized with the adoption by the United States and the USSR of the Nuclear Nonproliferation Treaty in 1968. By 1990, however, a number of small countries (including India, Pakistan, Israel, and South Africa) seemed to possess some nuclear capabilities.

Nuclear weapons in the hands of small states, however, did not represent the only challenge to world peace. Because of advances in the technology of warfare, highly destructive weapons such as antiaircraft and antitank guns had become cheaper and more mobile. Vietnam, Afghanistan, and Nicaragua provided striking indications of the fact that fighting forces without their own large industrial base, as long as they had some external sources of supply, could exact a high cost from a better armed adversary.

Other developments also pointed to the increasing spread of destructive military power. Some small states, for instance, were acquiring such highly potent devices as chemical weapons and ballistic missile delivery systems. A few, including Libya and Syria, were widely believed to be capable of using such weapons if they thought the use would damage U.S. interests.

Perhaps the most baffling security problem of all, however, was in the increasingly destructive powers of nonstate groups such as the Irish Republican Army and the Abu Nidal terrorists. Sometimes in collusion with friendly governments, sometimes on their own, these groups were using devices of increasing sophistication with which to threaten governments. By 1990 no satisfactory response to these deeply troubling problems had yet emerged.

Coping with Open Borders

In 1990 the United States and other countries were grappling with consequences of the increasing openness of their borders, responding with policies that were often contradictory and inconsistent. On the one hand, most governments were eager to promote the interests of their nationals as they sought to penetrate foreign markets and draw on foreign resources. On the other hand, most governments also felt a compelling need to maintain some measure of control over their national economies, in order to promote national security, encourage economic growth, and meet other national goals demanded by their electorates. The result was a highly confusing set of international policies, with some measures aimed at promoting greater openness while others were aimed at trying to maintain some degree of national control. For the United States, the contradictions were especially evident in the areas of international trade and international investment.

International Trade Policies

The year 1990 found the United States engaged in some of the most ambitious efforts it had ever undertaken to open up international markets. With the ratification of the U.S.–Canada Free Trade Agreement in 1988, the two countries were in the first stages of dismantling the restrictions affecting the flow of goods, services, and capital across their common border; inasmuch as each country ranked first as trading partner of the other, the significance of that measure was very substantial. At the same time, the U.S. government was launched on an ambitious agenda of negotiations in the General Agreement on Tariffs and Trade (GATT), aimed at opening up world markets in services and easing certain restrictions on foreign direct investment flows. The European Community's moves to eliminate the remaining internal barriers of its member states by 1992 seemed likely to precipitate a new wave of negotiations with the United States aimed at reducing external barriers at the same time.

Despite these ambitious undertakings, however, the United States was operating under a set of statutory provisions, contained in the Omnibus Trade and Competitiveness Act of 1988, that was more protectionist in potential effect than any trade act enacted in the prior half century. Under the terms of the 1988 law, threats became a dominant instrument of U.S. trade policy. The president was explicitly authorized and directed to assemble a list of restrictive trade practices followed by other governments and to deny those governments access to U.S. markets unless they responded satisfactorily to our complaints. In the same statute, the ability of aggrieved U.S. interests to press their cases for protection was increased in various ways, threatening to overwhelm the executive with a flood of cases.

Meanwhile, some U.S. observers noted that U.S. trading ties and other economic links with countries on the Pacific Rim were growing more rapidly than those with Europe, and that U.S. trade with Pacific Rim countries exceeded trade with Europe. Accordingly, they urged that the United States loosen its economic links to Europe and develop closer ties to the Pacific Rim countries. Proposals of this sort were usually vague in their details, so it was difficult to determine the feasibility and desirability of such a shift. In any event, the interests of the United States in Europe, when measured by transatlantic investments and security commitments, continued to be far greater than its interests in the Pacific Rim areas. Moreover, the continuing global character of U.S. economic, military, and political interests suggested that any substantial regionalization of its economic arrangements was unlikely.

International Financial Policies

Some of the confusing and contradictory elements that appeared in U.S. trade policies in 1990 also could be seen in emerging U.S. attitudes toward foreigners' investments in U.S. subsidiaries and branches.

The traditional position of the United States, vigorously promoted with missionary zeal in the 1950s and in the two decades following, had been to urge other nations to allow foreigners freely to set up businesses in their jurisdictions. With only a few limited exceptions, the U.S. position was that all nations should extend to foreign owned enterprises in their jurisdictions the same treatment they would accord to their own nationals.

However, as Japanese and European enterprises increased their business interests in the United States, official U.S. action became much more confused. In one celebrated case, U.S. authorities scared off a Japanese firm from acquiring control over a California-based computer firm. At about the same time, the Department of Defense, having financed a consortium devoted to research in the manufacture of computer chips, denied membership in the consortium to those firms operating in the United States that were controlled by foreigners. As usual, such measures were justified in the name of "defense"; but with Japanese firms the obvious target, the justification was widely seen as no more than a fig leaf.

Other evidences of uncertainty over the nature and status of foreign owned subsidiaries repeatedly surfaced. As foreign owned banks set up their subsidiaries and affiliates in different locations in the United States, American authorities found that the provisions that limited U.S. banks to doing business in a single state could not readily be applied to foreign owned banks. That realization added insult to injury, inasmuch as U.S. banks operating in some foreign countries were hemmed in by much greater restrictions than existed in the United States. As a result, the air was full of discussions whether "reciprocity" rather than "national treatment" should be the rule determining the rights of foreign owned banks and other foreign owned enterprises in the United States.

More important, however, was a growing realization that the trend to multinational structures in business enterprises and to the internationalization of capital markets placed substantial constraints on the capacity of governments to exercise effective controls over their own borders. Most U.S. officials had long since recognized the point with regard to the flow of technology across U.S. borders, and had largely resigned themselves to the fact that unilateral U.S. restrictions could only succeed in slowing up the flow for brief periods of time. Other governments were learning that capital controls were becoming increasingly impractical, undermined by the increasing efficiency of electronic communication and the internalization of transactions within multinational networks.

Doubts over the efficacy of unilateral governmental measures could be seen not only in programs of direct control, such as controls over the flow of technology and capital, but also in programs that sought indirectly to influence the economy through monetary and exchange rate policies. With the end of fixed exchange rates in 1971, governments began to make more frequent use of exchange rates and interest rates as policy instruments, hoping to promote national interests through changes in those rates. Eventually, however, it became evident that the internationalization of business and finance was tending to reduce the effectiveness of the exchange rate as a policy instrument. For example, U.S. efforts in the middle 1980s to lower the value of the dollar in order to improve the trade balance produced sluggish and disappointing results. Part of that disappointing response could be tracked to complex strategies by foreign firms, reflecting their commitment to hold a long-term position in the U.S. market; by operating their U.S. subsidiaries at reduced profit margins, they could offset some of the effects of the devaluation of the U.S. dollar.

In other situations, on the other hand, the intimate linkages between national capital markets tended to thwart unilateral governmental policies because of the highly sensitive reactions to price changes that such linkages fostered. When U.S. monetary authorities sought to tighten credit in the United States, for instance, banks that were part of an international network usually responded by borrowing dollars in other countries and lending them in the United States, a reaction that reduced the impact of the measures taken by the U.S. authorities. Similar reactions could be detected among European currencies as capital market controls were eased within the European Community.

The New Internationalism

The sense of enhanced openness and vulnerability that most governments were experiencing in 1990 produced a complex set of responses. Some of these were unilateral measures aimed at limiting transactions with other countries, such as imposing quotas on imports that threatened domestic industries. Some, however, took the form of new measures of cooperation with other countries to deal with common problems.

On economic issues, a number of the cooperative undertakings of 1990 were of a kind that could not easily have been envisaged in 1950. In that year, to be sure, some major international agreements and international institutions were already in existence, reflecting an emphasis of U.S. leaders on open global markets. The International Monetary Fund (IMF) and the World Bank had recently been created, and the General Agreement on Tariffs and Trade was just beginning to function.

Even in 1950, however, the emphasis on a global economic approach had been equivocal. Neither the IMF nor the World Bank was allowed to play much of a role in the reconstruction of Europe and Japan, an exercise that was conducted largely through the Marshall Plan and through benign occupation policies. And the GATT in practice was proving to be primarily an institution to promote tariff negotiations among the advanced industrialized countries, with developing countries largely excused from the agreement's undertakings. In the four decades from 1950 to 1990, there would be numerous reaffirmations of the fact that governments preferred to deal with their major economic issues in smaller groups composed of countries with which they shared strong common interests.

The most striking illustrations of new patterns of international cooperation in 1990 were provided by the twelve-nation European Community in Europe and the U.S.–Canada Free Trade Agreement. Each of these arrangements was distinguished by strong commitments and strong dispute-settlement machinery of a kind difficult to conceive in 1950.

In the various activities involving the flow of money across international borders, international cooperation among small groups of countries was especially extensive and varied.

One of the earliest manifestations of such cooperation had appeared quite early in the decades after 1950. As multinational enterprises developed their international networks of subsidiaries and affiliates, it soon became evident that the way in which the various national taxing authorities defined taxable profits would expose some of the global profits of these networks to double taxation. The threat of paying taxes to several different countries on a given dollar of profits drove multinational enterprises to support a series of bilateral agreements designed to reduce that risk.

Another manifestation of the same tendency toward cooperation appeared in the 1970s and 1980s, as international banks accepted a series of agreements among bank supervisory authorities aimed at tightening up the creditworthiness of international banks. In this case, the fear of the international banks and their governments was that the failure of any one of these banks could threaten the solvency of all the others. In the wings were proposals for more active collaboration among authorities concerned with the regulation of securities markets.

In addition to cooperating in these relatively narrow and specialized areas, the monetary authorities of North America, Europe, and Japan, taking cognizance of their vulnerability to changes in their exchange rates, were periodically taking joint action to try to deal with the vast flow of money that linked their respective economies. Joint efforts to limit the movements of foreign exchange rates grew relatively frequent. This type of cooperation, although informal and sporadic, was one of substantial significance for the future.

The new forms of cooperation among countries were not confined to economic issues alone. Environmental issues also were pushing governments toward collaborative efforts of an unusual kind. An agreement among several dozen countries to limit the use of gases that imperiled the ozone layer established a promising precedent for other such measures. International discussions aimed at controlling the greenhouse effect by limiting the discharge of hydrocarbons into the atmosphere were high on the global agenda, as were discussions of the effects of destroying tropical forests.

Even in the field of national security, developments were pushing governments toward some new measures of international collaboration. To be sure, as the cold war atmosphere receded, military alliances of a traditional kind such as NATO and the Warsaw Pact appeared to be weakening rather than strengthening. But the new dimensions of the threats presented by outlaw countries such as Libya and by nonstate terrorist groups appeared to be pushing governments toward closer collaboration in exchanges of information and surveillance.

In the case of the U.S. government, the increasing interaction among countries on issues of common interest posed a major problem of governance. Increasingly, the issues that were the subject of consultation, ranging from monetary affairs to the environment, were subjects deeply embedded in domestic politics. Under the division of powers that was a fundamental part of the U.S. system of checks and balances, the authority to deal with these issues was divided among the three branches of government. Increasingly, it was apparent that effective international discussion and negotiation would require closer collaboration between Congress and the executive. An obvious challenge facing policy makers in 1990 was to fashion more effective means for such collaboration.

2

Managing Change: The United States and Europe East and West

PETER W. LUDLOW

Introduction

During the second Reagan administration, Europe, East and West, changed profoundly. Before discussing U.S. interests in relation to Europe, it is necessary to assess the nature, the origins, the durability, and the eventual consequences of the changes that have occurred. The first part of

PETER W. LUDLOW is director of the Center for European Policy Studies in Brussels, Belgium, a position he has held since 1981. In 1986 he was a member and rapporteur of the European Community–ASEAN High Level Working Party on EC investments in ASEAN. Mr. Ludlow was professor of history at the European University Institute in Florence from 1976 to 1981, and a lecturer in history at the University of London from 1966 to 1975. He is the author of numerous publications on international history and politics in the twentieth century.

this chapter is therefore devoted to a discussion of the situation in Europe.

The principal arguments can be briefly summarized. In the first place, the changes that are currently occurring in both East and West, though dramatic in quality, are not in any way surprising or superficial. They are logical outcomes of lengthy processes of adjustment. Such a conclusion does not imply that they will without question proceed along a predictable course: it does, however, imply that there is real momentum behind both reform movements and, furthermore, that even if the particular programs currently being pursued or the particular group of leaders currently in charge should for one reason or another falter, the underlying pressures that gave birth to them will remain.

A further theme is also important. At root, both reform processes are political in character, even though in origin they owe much to economic and social forces, and in consequence they will alter the economic and social landscape. This point is relatively easily grasped in relation to the Soviet Union. It is perhaps not so readily understood in relation to 1992. In retrospect, however, the real breakthrough during the first Delors Commission was not the drafting or even the approval of the famous White Paper sketching out a plan to create a single market by 1992, but the changes in the political system brought about by the Single European Act, the adoption of which was facilitated by agreement on the White Paper. The reality with which the United States is confronted in Western Europe is not simply a more competitive economy, but a new political entity.

The implications of these changes for U.S. policy are considered later. In keeping with the emphasis on the systemic character of the changes within Europe, discussion in this section is primarily concerned with principles and with framework-creating initiatives that can foster an environment within which U.S.–European relations can develop, despite numerous, unavoidable strains arising from rapid change. Hormones and agricultural subsidies, pasta and public procurement are not forgotten: detailed solutions to these and other technical problems can, however, be sought and found only if an underlying community of interest between the two sides of the Atlantic is clearly established and structures for managing the relationship are created. These latter are the focus of this chapter.

Systemic Change in Europe, East and West

1992 and Beyond

There are still those, not only outside the European Community (EC), but also within it, who apparently believe that the new euphoria in the European Community is the result of a fluke or a confidence trick, and that at some stage in the near future, the new-found momentum will begin to slow down and matters will revert to the former, semiparalyzed state. While it would be equally superficial to pretend that the present process is irreversible and that the European Community finds itself on a moving staircase leading effortlessly and painlessly toward European union, it is nevertheless important to recognize that the "new Community" has been emerging for at least two decades, and that the present phase can and should be seen as a logical consequence of internal developments in Europe and fundamental changes in the global system.

There is neither space nor need in this chapter to rehearse at length arguments that I have developed in another essay ("Beyond 1992: Europe and its Western Partners." CEPS Paper nr 38 Brussels, January 1989). The following points are, however, essential to the theme of the present chapter.

The Linkages between Change in Europe and the Evolution of the Global System. The infant European Community was launched in the context of an international system dominated globally by East-West rivalry and characterized in the West by

U.S. hegemony. The new European Community had from the beginning a high policy mission: to unite countries previously at war and in doing so to lay the bases of a European union. The agenda of the new Community was, however, essentially concerned with low policy issues: trade, agriculture, transport, coal, and steel. Macroeconomic and monetary issues, and still more foreign and security questions, were discussed and elaborated within the alliance framework, in a dialogue between client states and the alliance leader. Even trade issues, in which the EC institutions quickly established their right to speak for Europe, were circumscribed by a system in which the United States, as the dominant element in world trade, was the main rule setter.

Another characteristic of this system must also be mentioned: its systemic bilateralism. The most important outward and visible signs of the alliance were, of course, the multilateral institutions. Much of the most important policy formulation took place, however, in bilateral discussions between the leader and its clients. The prototype for this system had been worked out during the Second World War by the Americans and the British. It was indeed, in many respects, a system "made in Britain," and it was peculiarly useful to the British. In due course, however, it was emulated elsewhere. Bilateral relations between Bonn and Washington, Rome and Washington, and even Paris and Washington exceeded in significance any bilateral or multilateral groupings of a purely European character for a very long time.

In the course of the late 1960s and early 1970s, this rather simple global system began to dissolve. There are various elements in the process, and each merits extended treatment. The most important, however, are:

- The changing role of the United States within the Western system.
- The search for accommodation between the superpowers, which despite untidy phases has been a more or less continuous theme of the 1970s and 1980s.

- The emergence of new political and economic power centers, notably in the Pacific and Western Europe itself.
- The technology-driven globalization of manufacturing processes and the financial markets, which, quite apart from anything else, reduced—for good and ill—the capacity of individual governments or international organizations to influence the course of events.

The EC's history in the 1970s and 1980s can be interpreted in large measure as a response to this changing international environment.

The Emergence of a "New Community." The initial impact of global destabilization in the late 1960s and 1970s on the European Community was almost entirely negative. The EC's institutions themselves came under severe strains, as member states were confronted with international monetary instability, inflation, and increasing signs of a breakdown of the consensus on foreign and security policies. Nontariff barriers were hastily erected as substitutes for the tariff barriers that had been so spectacularly abolished in the 1960s, and phony currency arrangements were made to preserve the fiction of an integrated market in agriculture. Political rhetoric in the Pompidou-Heath-Brandt era proclaimed the need for the Community to develop bold new policy initiatives. A high policy Community could not, however, be constructed so quickly on the bases of inexperience and disorder.

This crisis of the 1970s seriously scarred both the internal morale and external reputation of the Community, with the result that even insiders remained for long pessimistic about the ability of Europe to cope with the new global order. Looking back, however, it is possible to discern the slow and painful emergence of a "new Community" in the wake of and as a response to the international crisis. At least six themes merit particular mention:

- The formalization of heads of government and state participation in the Community process, through the launching of the European Council. Without the involvement of those holding the most important positions of power in Western Europe, there would have been little hope of an extension of the Community's competence to monetary policy, foreign policy, and security issues.

- The successful establishment of the European Monetary System (EMS), without which 1992 could not have been conceived at all.

- Changing attitudes toward the role of government, which, in terms of the Community's own internal balance, paved the way for a redefinition of both the extent and limits of government at the Community level itself. The changing parameters of the Community's discussions of its own budget, and more generally of the role of public expenditure in European integration, are among the clearest measures of this evolution.

- The emergence in the Davignon era of a new, creative coalition between business elites and the Community institutions, which had a major impact both on the genesis of new policies—particularly in research and development and in the Single Market plan itself—and on the implementation of them. Business representatives, provoked by global competition, turned to the Community as the only framework capable of providing them with the "home base" that they needed.

- The consolidation of a regional bloc extending from the Nordic countries to the Mediterranean, both through formal acts, such as the three enlargements and the Luxembourg agreement between the European Community and the European Free Trade Association (EFTA) in 1984, and through the inner momentum of the integration process.

- The tentative but nevertheless real progress toward the definition of the Community's external identity and security interests in a medley of institutions, including in particular European Political Cooperation (EPC), the revamped Western European Union (WEU), and the Independent European Programmes Group (IEPG).

The Single Market plan is thus only part of the emergent structure. It depended on other elements for its conception; it will require their further maturity if it itself is to be more than a sickly infant.

The Political Character of the Integration Process. Some observers, both inside and outside, still seem to believe that the European Community is merely a rather highly developed consequence of multilateral trade negotiations. This is a serious underestimation of both the original motivation of those who launched the venture in the 1950s and the dynamics of the new phase. The real change that has taken place in the last three to four years is not to be found in the White Paper of 1985, outlining a plan to create a single market by 1992, but in the modification of the EC's political system brought about in the so-called Single European Act.

The case successfully argued by the commission president and his colleagues in 1985, that a program as ambitious as the Single Market plan could not be realized without radical changes in the Community's own way of doing things and in particular without the introduction of majority voting, assumes greater significance still as we move toward 1992. The process could not have been launched without political innovation: once in train, however, it has itself already significantly altered the balance of power between nation states and the Community institutions.

Looking still further ahead, it is difficult if not impossible to conceive of a fully functioning single market without Community institutions that are competent, not simply in the relatively well-defined sphere of the market itself, but also in economic and monetary affairs and in external policies. As the development of the Community's external relations in 1988 proved, progress toward 1992 had a profound impact on the Community's standing with its Western allies and partners, and its Eastern neighbors. By the same token, the Community's external policies are already of much greater import than "commercial policy" in the traditional sense.

Sustainability and Timing. It would be naive to pretend that success is certain. But the progress so far (and in particular the fundamental commitments already taken, not only by political actors but also by economic agents, on the assumption that the process will be successful) coupled with the continuing external rationale that gave rise to the new realities in the first place suggest that the momentum is more or less irreversible. There may well be some untidy political crises, involving in particular the United Kingdom. U.K. opposition will not, however, disrupt the exercise, and given the United Kingdom's own in-depth involvement in the day-to-day workings of the system, it will have no option over time but to fall in line.

In assessing the relevance of these changes to U.S. strategic planning it is, of course, also important to comment on the likely order of events, and to arrive at a very rough sense of timing. One can only speculate, but it seems quite likely that by the mid- to late 1990s, the single market and economic and monetary union elements of the package will be in place, and that the core European Community (including possibly one or two new members) will have negotiated a broad institutional framework for the management of the regional bloc as a whole, including the EFTA and the Mediterranean states. These developments would then provide the basis for a *subsequent* reorganization of European defense and Europe's contribution to the alliance. In any realistic scenario, however, major advances in these areas can happen only after the completion of the EC's economic programs and the further definition of its "political" identity. This has important implications for the U.S. administration's discussion of burden sharing and other alliance related issues.

Upheaval in the Soviet Union and Eastern Europe

An exhaustive analysis of the origins, character, and prospects of the changes currently taking place in the Soviet Union and Eastern Europe is clearly beyond the scope of this chapter.

The purpose is more modest: to identify those elements in the situation that directly affect the West or that offer challenges to harmonious U.S.–European management of the change. The argument can be considered under three headings.

The Principal Challenge to the West Over the Next Fifteen Years Will Stem Not from Soviet and Eastern European Strength, but from Their Weakness. This assertion is not, it should be stressed, tantamount to saying that the Soviet threat in a military sense has vanished or will vanish overnight. On the contrary, there has been, and there probably will continue to be, a rather obvious decalage between political and economic developments and changes in the Soviet Union's military posture and capabilities. We are still a very long way away from a situation in which we can in military terms relax our guard or indulge in the luxury of uncoordinated alliance policies. The fact is, however, that the Gorbachev phenomenon is more a monument to failure than a guarantee of rejuvenation.

The bare statistics on Soviet economic growth since 1965 (Table 1) provide one fairly comprehensive measure of weakness. These general perspectives can be complemented by the regular flow of gloomy information about specific sectors, about the budget deficit, and about external trade and debt.

Mere statistics are, however, only indicators of the crisis. The reality lies much deeper, in the bankruptcy of ideology, and in the mismatch between visions of what might, or ought to be, and the grim realities of institutional rigidity and societal backwardness, inherited from pre-Communist regimes and compounded by communism. The success of the Gorbachev experiment remains totally uncertain: the consequences of failure are, however, unlikely to be a return to a self-confident—or at the very least ruthlessly effective—dictatorship, so much as still greater weakness, vulnerability, and degradation than exist today. The principal problem for the West in the coming decades will not be to maintain balance, but to cope with imbalance.

Table 1. Soviet Economic Growth Since 1965

	1966–70	1971–75	1976–80	1981–85	1985	1986	1987
A. Soviet official measures							
NMP produced	7.7	5.7	4.2	3.5	3.5[a]	4.1[a]	2.3
NMP utilized	7.1	5.1	3.9	3.2	3.1[a]	3.6[a]	
Gross industrial output	8.5	7.4	4.4	3.6	3.9	4.9	3.8
Gross agricultural output[b]	3.9	2.4	1.7	1.1	0.0	5.1	0.2
Investment[b]	7.4	7.2	5.2	3.2	3.0	8.0	4.7
Capital stock	7.5	7.9	6.8	6.0	5.5	5.3	
Electric power	7.9	7.0	4.5	3.6	3.5	3.6	4.1
Oil, coal, and gas	5.2	5.4	4.2	2.5	2.4	4.6	3.1
B. CIA estimates[c]							
GNP	5.1	3.0	2.3	1.9	0.8	3.8	
Industrial output	6.4	5.5	2.7	1.9	2.0	3.1	
Agricultural output	3.6	−0.6	0.8	2.1	−1.7	7.3	
Investment	5.5	4.3	4.3	3.4	2.1	6.0	
Capital stock	7.4	8.0	6.9	6.2	5.8	5.5	
Labor (human-hours)	2.0	1.7	1.2	0.7	0.4	0.4	

Notes. General: All output series, and the investment and capital stock series are, in principle, in constant prices, i.e., they denote "real" changes. The Soviet official series, however, are known to contain an element of hidden inflation and therefore are upward biased. See also note a.
a: Soviet reported growth rates for 1985 and 1986 are more than usually upward biased. See Philip Hanson, RL Research Report, No. 76/87, February 26, 1987, and Jan Vanous in PlanEcon Report, February 11, 1987.
b: For five-year periods, the growth rates shown are those between the total for the period and the total for the preceding five-year period.
c: At 1982 ruble factor cost. 1986 figures are preliminary.

Sources: Narodnoe khozyaistvo SSSR (various years); *Pravda,* January 24, 1988; CIA, *Handbook of Economic Statistics 1986;* CIA and DIA, *Gorbachev's Modernization Program: A Status Report,* Paper prepared for the Subcommittee on Security Economics of the U.S. Congress Joint Economic Committee, March 19, 1987; "The Gorbachev Challenge and European Security," A Report from the European Strategy Group.

The Quality and Pace of the Eastern Bloc's Response to Their Crisis Will Be Determined Principally By Internal Factors. This point is probably self-evident: it is nevertheless worth emphasizing, since it has important practical implications. Two merit particular mention.

The first is that, as events have shown since the Gorbachev induced change in atmosphere, the capacity of Eastern bloc countries to adjust to new challenges and possibilities varies greatly. There cannot, at the moment, be any serious question of a break in the Warsaw Pact in military terms, but there is already ample evidence to show that social and economic progress will not be uniform. The failure of the Soviet Union to create any genuine economic unity in the East during its years of undisputed hegemony will therefore bear fruit in increasingly divergent performance and policy, not only between states that are formally sovereign, but also within the Soviet Union itself.

How and where the differences will emerge will depend on a variety of factors. In certain cases, such as Hungary and Bulgaria, divergence could probably have been predicted anyway, given the different economic and social structures of the two countries. The differing responses of East Germany and Hungary, by contrast, have more to do with internal politics and external security perceptions than with basic economic or social capacities. Within the Soviet Union itself, there will also be serious tensions and differences, with the Baltic states as obvious candidates for special treatment: a Finlandization in reverse.

These differences *within* the Eastern bloc have important implications for policy design in the West, as shown by the recent EC–Hungary agreement, which is at one and the same time a pat on the back for the most progressive Eastern European economy and an inducement to others to emulate Hungary.

The second corollary of the basic proposition is also significant. There are limits to what the West can or should try to do.

There is nothing inherently wrong about thinking through a grand, Marshall-like plan for the East, but Western willingness to help on a generous scale will be less important in the long run than the East's capacity to absorb the transfers of capital resources. The experience of Western bankers and industrialists who participated in the first wave of Western investment in the East in the late 1960s and 1970s is a relatively venerable, but nevertheless useful, illustration of the difficulties that arise when eager investors become enmeshed in a rigid and inflexible system.

Finland's experience in the 1980s is a more recent, and perhaps still better, guide. Obliged by the terms of its bilateral understanding with the Soviet Union to export to the Soviet Union only as much, in value terms, as it can import, Finland has an obvious incentive to buy as much as it can. In the bad old days of high energy prices, the problem was not acute. Finland sold sophisticated products and bought in exchange, at world prices, oil and other energy related purchases. With the fall in world oil prices, Finland obviously hoped that it could buy other Soviet goods, so that its own level of exports could be maintained. Despite an extensive and extremely knowledgeable army of experts mandated to search high and low for suitable things to buy, the Finns could not reduce the heavy share of energy in the overall Soviet export package, and as a result were forced to accept a significant reduction in their own exports to the Soviet Union. To meet the problem the Finns stepped up the amount of credit that they were ready to make available to the Soviets, but both inside and outside experts seriously question whether, in the short run at any rate, the Soviet system itself can respond.

The Finnish case is a microcosm of a more general problem, and so, perhaps, a useful reminder to those who worry about the increasing volume of Western European credits, that constraints in the marketplace itself will probably provide the best discipline against unwise magnanimity.

History, Common Sense, and Recent Soviet and Eastern Bloc Policies Suggest that Western Europe Will Have a Special Role in the Opening Up of the East to Western Economic Penetration. This is a very large theme indeed, which merits extensive consideration. The trade figures provide some indication of the trend of events (Tables 2 and 3). They also confirm the special place within Western Europe of the Federal Republic of Germany.

There is a growing amount of evidence to suggest that Soviet leaders, and the leaders of the more advanced Eastern European countries, place a high priority on the development of special relations with the rest of Europe. One indication can be found in the switch in Soviet policy toward the European Community since Mikhail Gorbachev came to power. It has been particularly evident in the external policies of the Council for Mutual Economic Assistance (CMEA or COMECON),

Table 2.

	Exports from EC to Eastern Europe and Soviet Union (Millions of ECU)		
	1985	*1986*	*1987*
EC 12	23.437	20.188	19.160
FRG	9.589	9.194	8.567
France	3.818	2.795	2.665
Italy	3.446	2.925	3.103
U.K.	1.988	1.735	1.569
	Imports to EC from Eastern Europe and Soviet Union		
EC 12	33.896	24.759	24.423
FRG	10.250	8.363	7.434
France	4.539	3.879	3.700
Italy	6.493	4.230	4.912
U.K.	2.903	2.445	2.594

Source: Eurostat.

Table 3.

U.S. Merchandise Trade with USSR and Eastern Europe Millions of dollars (Dollar = +/− 0.9 ECU)			
Exports	*1985*	*1986*	*1987*
USSR	2.423	1.248	1.480
Eastern Europe	792	742	746
Imports			
USSR	443	605	470
Eastern Europe	1.671	1.600	1.651

Source: U.S. Department of Commerce.

which is, of course, totally dominated by the USSR. As early as May 1985, Gorbachev raised the possibility of a new relationship between the CMEA and the EC. Three years later, on June 15, 1988, official relations were established between the CMEA and the European Community after a negotiation in which by common consent the CMEA conceded more in political terms than it received. Since the summer of 1988, one of several growth industries in Brussels has been the opening of Eastern bloc embassies accredited to the Community as such.

Other indications of the general pattern abound. The newly established Soviet Institute for European Affairs, for example, has launched a series of studies of 1992, and preliminary conclusions aired by some of those involved suggest that the Soviet Union is likely to find a more congenial partner in its pursuit of modernization in the European Community than in either the United States or Japan. Nor is the European Community the only focus of attention. Both Yugoslavia and Hungary, which have increasingly important relations with Brussels, have reportedly been sounding out some of the EFTA states about the prospects of association and even eventual adhesion.

In any historical or geopolitical perspectives, these developments are not particularly surprising. They do, however, raise questions that the United States and its Western partners will be well advised to treat together, rather than apart.

U.S. Policy Toward the New Europe

The previous section has sketched the context in which the Bush administration will have to develop its European policy. It is a highly dynamic and, by definition, uncertain environment. The only sure assumption on which we would be wise to build is that there will be ample opportunity for misunderstanding and friction between the United States and its European allies over issues both great and small.

Disputes comparable to those that have sprung up over the past thirty years about chickens, pasta, hormones, and sundry other mundane, not to say homely, companions of our two-way trade will doubtless recur. They must to some extent be seen as an inevitable consequence of increasing interdependence. Viewed in another perspective, however, they can be regarded as safety valves in a much deeper process of adjustment from a hegemonial alliance to a partnership between economic blocs of more or less equal strength and potential.

As progress toward 1992 quickens, and as the wider implications of the Single European Act become apparent, it seems difficult to believe that the argument will not become more wide-ranging and more strategic in character. The year 1988, in which the U.S. administration and the media discovered "fortress Europe," provided a foretaste of what is to come. If it is relatively easy to puncture that particular image, it would be naive to pretend that the demolition of one myth will pave the way for an era of relaxed comradeship and constructive cooperation. In a process as highly political as the current reconstruction of Western Europe, there will be losers as well as winners, costs as well as benefits, within and without.

Historical parallels should not be pushed too far. It is nevertheless salutory to recall the history of Anglo–U.S. relations in the first half of this century, and more particularly in the climactic decade of the 1940s. A strong alliance and a special relationship may in the end have overridden rivalries and conflicts: they were not, however, forged without them. In a redistribution of power and roles of the kind that is currently under way between the United States and Europe, it would be strange if we did not witness latter-day versions of the bruising conflicts over principle and turf that went on in the 1940s between Keynes and White, the U.K. Treasury and the U.S. Treasury, Wall Street and the City, the State Department and the Foreign Office.

Against this background, it would seem more relevant and useful in this chapter to concentrate on general principles and framework-setting initiatives rather than to embark on detailed discussion of how we might defuse disputes over agricultural subsidies, reciprocity, inward investment, and all the other discrete issues that either already occupy or in the near future will occupy the attention of policy makers on both sides of the Atlantic. The argument can be advanced under five headings.

Western European Integration and Soviet and Eastern European Reform Are in the U.S. Interest

Twenty years ago, the first part of the heading to this section would have seemed entirely superfluous. Successive American administrations in the 1950s and 1960s affirmed their belief in the desirability of a united Europe, and at several critical moments, gave active encouragement to those who wanted to go further and faster. Today, as the "fortress Europe" syndrome has demonstrated, the assumption of an underlying community of interest can no longer be taken for granted.

In the light of the historical analysis provided earlier, this new anxiety is not particularly surprising. A European pillar in a period of undisputed American hegemony was at best a convenient prop, but perhaps in reality, as Christoph Bertram of *Die Zeit* recently remarked, "a contradiction in terms." The stakes in the 1980s are different and higher. The desirability of a strong Western European partner must therefore be justified rather than assumed. The arguments are, nevertheless, fairly simple.

• In a global economy in which there is no longer an undisputed leader—and there is little prospect of creating at world level the sovereignty-infringing and legally binding institutional environment currently upheld by the nation states—regional blocs or continental-size economies are essential elements in a stable economic order. The amount of mutual surveillance and shared government already achieved through the European Monetary System (EMS) involves sacrifices of sovereignty that are, even in European terms, unacceptable to British Prime Minister Margaret Thatcher, and in global terms, for the time being at any rate, unachievable. The sharp reduction of exchange rate volatility and the concomitant convergence of economic policy and performance that have resulted from the creation of the EMS have not only benefited the participating countries, but significantly simplified the tasks of global management.

A similar argument can be advanced in the trade sphere. The 1992 program is not in contradiction with the agreed objectives of the Uruguay Round: it is in many important respects in advance of them. The fact is that in economies as interdependent as those of the EC–EFTA–Mediterranean zone, advanced experiments in common regulation and government are both more necessary and more feasible than they are at the global level, where, despite the immense increase in world trade, trade linkages are more modest and the opportunities for devising adequate institutional arrangements more remote. It is appropriate and in many respects useful for the United States to highlight hidden protectionism in the 1992 enterprise: it is short-sighted in the extreme to suggest that the effort to provide better government in a regional bloc that already exists is by definition destructive of a liberal world economy. On the contrary, regional blocs are building blocks.

• A genuine European pillar, involving in effect the extension
of the Community system to matters hitherto regarded as
the preserve of the alliance, is indispensable for the maintenance of the alliance itself and the preservation of order and
balance in Europe, not to mention the world. Adherence to
the broad notion of a European pillar in the context of the
West-West relationship is now almost universal. Acceptance
of what this means in practice is rather less developed on
both sides of the Atlantic. It would however be extremely
difficult if not impossible to imagine a genuine European
pillar except on the basis of the European Community.
Other stopgap solutions such as the IEPG or the WEU are
fundamentally flawed by the inadequacy of their juridical
status, while lesser solutions still, such as bilateral or trilateral arrangements between the "principal powers," can at
best only serve as catalysts of Western European unity, and
at worst simply perpetuate the asymmetry that has lain at the
heart of the Western Alliance since 1941 and which is, in
terms of the burden-sharing debate, its fundamental problem. If, therefore, the United States is serious about burden
sharing, it must be serious about Western European integration.

• The implications for the alliance of changes in the East point
in the same direction. Unless, very naively, one assumes that
Kant's perpetual peace has broken out all over, it is absolutely essential that Western solidarity be maintained as a
precondition of magnanimous management of evolution in
the East. A Western alliance consisting of one leader and
fifteen sovereign but more or less client states is for many
obvious reasons much more vulnerable than an alliance
based on two, three, or four decision-making cores. The
point has been highlighted in the post–INF (intermediate
nuclear forces) debate within Germany and between Germany and its Western allies. Impassioned calls to order from
Washington, stirring noises from London, and seductive
overtures from Paris are no substitute for a Western European structure in which the Federal Republic is firmly
lodged.

- Global perspectives too point in the same direction. After two decades in which the two superpowers have not only failed in their self-assigned roles as world police officers, but have also been seriously bruised as a result, there is a manifest need to overhaul the machinery for maintaining world order. A security council of which the core membership is still determined by the outcome of the Second World War is hardly an adequate basis on which to build. Given its economic and military strength, Western Europe clearly belongs to the inner group in any future order: given their individual economic and military strengths, it is equally clear that the British and the French do not.
- The advantages of changes in the Soviet Union and more generally in the Eastern bloc, which push the societies concerned toward greater openness, economically and politically, and as a result toward greater aptitude for global partnership in political and economic affairs, are presumably self-evident.

The Scope and Limits
of U.S. Power and Influence

The interest of the United States in Western European integration and orderly change in the East may be obvious: the limitations of U.S. power and influence are, however, no less important. In a country whose political culture encourages its leaders to be activist, and whose postwar history has accustomed them to leadership, counsels of caution may be unwelcome. American preeminence in the Western Alliance is not in question. So long as global security rests on nuclear deterrence and the American-Canadian economy maintains its superiority, by most important measures, to the economy of EC Twelve, the United States will and indeed must have a special place. Backward-looking calls to American "leadership," which were such a feature of official and nonofficial U.S. comment during the transitional period between the Reagan and Bush administrations, are not, however, a proper basis for policy, particularly as regards Europe. Given their ubiquity, it is somewhat arbitrary to fasten on two examples of the genre. Two cases can, however, be mentioned purely by way of illustration.

The first comes from an important and in many ways very enlightened report for the Pentagon on burden sharing by Thomas Callaghan in August 1988:

American leadership is paramount. Europeans cannot provide it for the simple reason that there is no Europe: no European political entity: no European military entity: no European entity with a competence in defence matters. Efforts to pool Europe's defence-industrial resources within one or another European institution have not been successful. . . . They never will be, unless or until the United States provides the creative, catalytic leadership.

In the light of the evidence discussed earlier in this chapter, the dismissal of Europe is, to say the least, premature: in the light of the intractable problems that lie in the way of Western European cooperation in armaments manufacture, the suggestion that somehow or other an American wand can achieve what the Europeans cannot is somewhat superficial. The restructuring of the European defense industry is already under way, thanks not so much to efforts within the North Atlantic Treaty Organization (NATO) as to the side-effects of developments within the European Community: its successful conclusion will, by the same token, depend far more on the extension of the EC's powers to the defense domain than on anything that Washington may decree.

Early statements by members of the Bush administration suggested that a proper sense of the limits of American power in its Western European "backyard" may not yet prevail in government itself. One need only cite the extraordinary suggestion by the secretary of commerce that the U.S. administration should be given a seat at the Community's deliberations about the Single Market.

As subsequent paragraphs will suggest, there is undoubtedly a role for skillful and subtle American diplomacy during the lifetime of the Bush administration. As far as Europe is concerned, however, there are two absolutely fundamental constraints. The first is one of time, the second one of substance.

The substantive point was well made by President Jacques Delors in his speech to the European Parliament in January 1989:

. . . our vision is of a "European Village" where understanding would reign, where economic and cultural activities would develop in mutual trust. But if I were asked to depict that Village today, I would see in it a House called the "European Community." We are its sole architects; we are the keepers of its keys; but we are prepared to open its doors to talk with our neighbours.

This is not arrogance: it is common sense. If the European construction is not made by Europeans, it will lack the legitimacy that alone can sustain it.

The question of timing is in a way still more important. Anybody who has followed developments in the European Community closely in the late 1980s must be impressed by the speed with which developments are taking place. There is still, however, some way to go even in terms of the internal market. More important still, from the point of view of global or alliance imbalances, completion of the 1992 program is only part of the story. U.S. interest may require a European pillar: politics cannot and will not deliver on it for several years to come, even on the most optimistic assumptions. American leaders legitimately anxious to reconstruct the global village will have to accept, therefore, that the European hamlet, not to mention the Western European house within it, is still in the hands of the architects and builders. Impatience could be helpful: overdone, it could be damaging.

This section would not be complete, however, if it ended on a purely negative note. While it is crucially important that the limits of American policy be acknowledged, there is within these limits a continuing leadership role. The United States *is* still a global power in ways that neither the European Community nor Japan is. Whereas, however, in an earlier generation the power balance was quite asymmetrical, it is now more even. The central function of U.S. leadership must therefore be to encourage a responsible and wide-ranging discussion of what partnership in global management really means.

Much of the trouble in the debate about burden sharing stems from the fact that U.S. allies do not know what the United States really wants to share. The greatest single contribution that the Bush administration could make to the revitalization of the extended Western Alliance would therefore be to communicate to its partners its vision of the world and its understanding of the proper roles of its allies.

This is in many ways a greater challenge to U.S. leadership than any that confronted previous administrations, whose power base ensured that their preferences and priorities were taken seriously by their allies. In the very different global environment in which we find ourselves, the United States must rely on persuasion still more than on the powers inherent in an asymmetrical relationship. It is not, however, an impossible challenge. Anybody who has observed the Community's own discussions of its global role in the last year at close quarters must be aware how sensitive in reality its leaders are to external pressure, particularly from the leader of the Western Alliance, and how anxious they are to clarify their position as "world partners." If in the new era, the administration starts out on the assumption that what is happening in Western Europe is in its interests, the dialogue can be fruitful and the changes that it brings about durable.

The Need for a Political Strategy

U.S. policy toward Western Europe has been based on a double-track approach, which reserved discussions of monetary and security policies to the intergovernmental machinery of the alliance and its various multilateral offspring. Discussions with the European Community as such have dealt, for most of the EC's thirty-year history, with trade, agriculture, and the old low policy agenda. The relaunching of the European Community in the 1970s and 1980s has rendered this tidy distinction obsolete. There is therefore an urgent need for the U.S. administration to reexamine the ways in which it deals with the European Community and its member states.

It would be presumptuous of a European to suggest how relations between the Departments of State, Treasury, Commerce, Agriculture, the National Security Council, and the Special Trade Representative should be coordinated. Suffice to say that the issues currently and potentially at stake in the relationship between the United States and the European Community stretch far beyond the competence of trade or agricultural specialists. Suggestions that the State Department might consider the creation of a special section to deal with "1992" are encouraging, as long as those concerned accept from the outset that what is involved is much more than the implementation of the White Paper.

Internal reorganization could very usefully be accompanied by an external initiative toward the European Community itself. In recent years, the artificial exclusion of high policy questions from the agenda in the regular meetings between the U.S. administration and the EC president and his senior commissioners has been ignored. This evolution is welcome and natural. It is not, however, of itself sufficient to ensure an adequate political dialogue between the European Community and the United States, because competence for the external relations of the Community is still divided between the Commission and the national foreign ministries grouped together in European Political Cooperation.

Under the terms of the Single European Act, the Commission and the presidency are required to ensure that the external policies of the European Community and the policies agreed in European Political Cooperation are consistent. Practice still, however, falls short of the ideal. In the last resort, the situation can be improved only by the European Community itself. The U.S. administration could, however, increase the likelihood of greater coherence in the EC's external policies by reviving an idea that has been put forward several times in the last ten to fifteen years. It would involve the establishment of a new consultative mechanism between the administration on the one hand and the EC's foreign ministers and the Commission on the other. The object would be to inject a political perspective into EC–U.S. discussions.

A body of this kind could prove an invaluable instrument at times of trade "war." It could also provide the basis for the development of common EC–U.S. positions in relation to the General Agreement on Tariffs and Trade (GATT), North-South questions, and, by no means least, the management of change in the East. Looking still further ahead, it could prepare the ground for an eventual reorganization of the summit structure away from its present historically understandable but politically illogical basis in the four larger European states plus the Commission and the member states. By the same token, it could be highly useful when the reorganization of Europe in NATO becomes a practical possibility.

In short, a common U.S.–EC council composed on the EC side of both the Commission and the Council of Ministers could prove exactly the kind of flexible and adaptable instrument that both sides of the Atlantic need to cope with an already wide, but widening, agenda. It would not of course replace the existing machinery for consultation and crisis management. It would, on the contrary, strengthen it.

Greater politicization of the EC–U.S. relationship could be advanced in other ways too. The function and strength of the U.S. Mission in Brussels, for example, almost certainly require review in the light of the new dynamism at the Community level. A U.S. initiative in this direction might, incidentally, have the entirely welcome effect of provoking the Community itself to look again at its own representation in Washington, which in several ways too is hardly relevant to the task that it ought to be performing in the new era. Another obvious area with scope for widening and deepening of contact is the Congress-Parliament relationship. There has been a marked increase in contact between the two institutions during recent years, but it must be questioned whether even so the present state of affairs is appropriate to the new political realities and in particular to the enhanced role of the European Parliament in the political process.

The Dangers of Bilateralism
and in Particular of the
Anglo-American Special Relationship

The suggestions advanced in previous paragraphs are not intended to imply that individual member states, and more particularly the larger ones, will rapidly cease to play an important part in transatlantic relations or in the world at large. On the contrary, we as Europeans, and therefore the United States as a partner, will have to live with a somewhat uncomfortable and not entirely transparent two-tier system for some time to come. There is, however, all the difference in the world between perpetuating and consolidating the systemic bilateralism that the British, with American agreement, devised in the 1940s and the maintenance of good relations with powerful members of a Community political system in which member states have a very powerful voice.

The issue can be seen most clearly in relation to the archetypal bilateral relationship between Washington and London. Properly handled, the special relationship can be an asset to the Community as a whole. If, however, its significance is over-estimated, it can become an obstacle to the construction of the Community. The illusions have usually been of British origin, but they have undoubtedly been fed by Washington's apparent readiness to play along. The resultant strains have been more or less kept under control in EPC and elsewhere, but the matter could assume an altogether different significance if, as is not impossible, the United Kingdom decides to stand apart from important initiatives to strengthen economic and monetary cooperation or political cooperation.

The problem is not simply one of intergovernmental relations. For reasons that are obvious and totally natural, U.S. public opinion knows more about the United Kingdom than any other single member state. London is also an important source of information about what is going on elsewhere in Europe. British newspapers and television are accessible, and the principal U.S. media agencies are more strongly implanted in the British capital than anywhere else. Add to this London's continuing role as a financial center on a par with New York and Tokyo, and it is easy to see how American images of the European Community can be significantly influenced by British interpretation and preoccupations. The fact that London is only one of twelve EC capitals, and that its government, to some extent through its own preferences, is far from being the most important player in the EC political system, is easily overlooked.

In normal times, the "London squint," which affects even an outstanding and extremely pro-European newspaper like the *Financial Times,* is both manageable and natural. In a period of change as rapid and as significant as the late 1980s, however, when the British are protagonists as well as participants, the bias can be more dangerous. European visitors to the United States in the late 1980s were frequently jolted when they heard apparently well-informed Americans mouthing some of the emptier slogans about the European Community coined by British ministers and politicians. One should not, over thirty years after the Treaty of Rome, have to explain that the Commission is *not* socialist, and that whatever centralizing instincts may lurk in some Eurocrats' hearts, with a total work force of 15,000 officials, including translators, they hardly have the means, even if they had the will, to dominate national governments.

The administration is of course better equipped than even the best-informed private citizens to sift and weigh many different sources of information. But even at the intergovernmental level, there are biases built into the fabric of the alliance itself, notably but not exclusively in the NATO framework. The British *are* still in many ways *primus inter pares.*

The U.S.–EC relationship would be seriously weakened over coming years if as a result of these various biases the administration were in any way to imply that it was a matter of indifference if the United Kingdom were to seek a special status in monetary affairs or in other directions, as its European partners move toward closer cooperation and integration. As I

have argued elsewhere, the *principal* loser in any such development will undoubtedly be the United Kingdom itself, but the
Community as a whole would also be weaker. So too would the
U.S.–EC partnership. It would be difficult, and possibly even
counterproductive, for the administration to lean on the British as, in the days of hegemony, earlier administrations did,
but it would be even more dangerous if in the curious Indian
summer of the special relationship a U.S. administration were,
even involuntarily, to strengthen British feelings of separate-
ness.

The dangers of systemic bilateralism are not, however, confined to the Anglo-American relationship. In many respects
indeed, for quite different reasons, they may be even more
important in connection with the Federal Republic. The
United States (and other allies) frequently complain about
German "softness" on East-West issues, both economic and
political. For reasons that have already been rehearsed above,
the surest way to lock the Federal Republic into the Western
system lies in a strengthening and deepening of the EC's identity. Excessive dependence on bilateral pressure can only undermine the longer-term objectives.

Even two examples will not, however, suffice. The whole
Western system is shot through with bilateralism. An almost
perfect illustration is to be found in the armaments sector,
where many of the most significant ventures in transatlantic
collaboration are covered by separate memoranda of understanding between the U.S. government and the defense ministries of the European member states. The system, it should be
stressed, grew up in response to European preferences rather
than to American efforts to divide and rule. The Reagan administration actually tried to break the system down in 1983 by
proposing the replacement of the separate memoranda by one
general agreement to be administered through the IEPG. It
would be entirely appropriate for the Bush administration to
relaunch that particular proposal.

More generally, it would be highly desirable if, with due
regard to national sensitivities and political realities, the ad-

ministration were to encourage European member states to
break with bilateralism and move toward common negotiations and agreements across the whole spectrum of the U.S.–
European relationship.

U.S.–EC Collaboration in East-West Relations

The discussion of U.S. policy toward the Soviet Union and
Eastern Europe in the Gorbachev era must be firmly related to
the foregoing analysis of U.S.–West European relations. The
challenge posed by recent developments in the East constitutes the most important opportunity for and test of the U.S.–
EC relationship. Both sides have obvious, fundamental interests at stake, which are by no means identical. As the
undisputed Western superpower in the military balance, U.S.
policy has already determined and will continue to determine
the environment within which relations between Western and
Eastern Europe develop. That said, it is extremely important
that the United States for its part acknowledge the distinctive
intra-European elements in the East-West relationship and the
special role that the European Community and its member
states can play in encouraging developments in the East that
are in the long-term interests of the Western Alliance as a
whole.

Soviet and East European interest in cultivating special relations with Western Europe has already been referred to earlier. President Delors's references in his Strasbourg speech of
January 1988 to the European village show that it has not gone
unnoticed. Within the context of the alliance, however, the
opportunity is also a challenge. U.S. policy toward the development of close relationships between Western and Eastern
European states in the past has been relatively permissive in
practice but profoundly wary in tone. In principle at any rate,
the new phase is qualitatively quite different from anything
that has preceded it. An entirely new European architecture
involving in due course perhaps the adhesion of Hungary, Yugoslavia, and others to the EFTA, and, more generally, an im-

mense expansion of economic transactions and human contacts is now distinctly possible.

These arrangements must, by definition, be European in the first instance. The challenge on both sides of the Atlantic will, therefore, be to ensure that Europe's opportunity not endanger the integrity of the alliance but, if at all possible, benefit the Western system as a whole. The United States cannot be the front runner in this race: it is crucially important, however, that it be neither disqualified nor injured in the course of it.

In order to ensure that intolerable strains are not imposed, closer political cooperation of the kind referred to earlier will be absolutely vital. Existing rules, unwritten and written within the Coordinating Committee on Export Controls (COCOM) and outside it, will be called into question. Unilateral action by the Europeans would be short-sighted; high-handed efforts to restrain European initiatives by the United States would be counterproductive. Specialist exchanges about COCOM will require the supervision of nonspecialists with a strong sense of strategy and politics.

There is no reason, however, why the United States' own position should be solely or even primarily reactive. There is already ample evidence that American companies can and will exploit the opportunities for new business within the Soviet bloc. At the level of public policy, there is also, as Institute for International Economics director C. Fred Bergsten recently urged, a strong case for greeting efforts by the Soviet Union and its client states to link up with the Western, multilateral system with sympathy and flexibility. It is scarcely conceivable that the Soviet Union or its Eastern European satellites could in any meaningful sense become full members of the GATT, the International Monetary Fund (IMF), or any other Western multilateral organization in the near future. This does not, however, exclude early association with them, along with lines already established in the case of China. Report after report from the East confirms that there is an almost touching anxiety to learn: no better way could be imagined than by association, observation, and contact.

If the United States were to take a lead in working out the
practical arrangements, this would, quite apart from anything
else, reduce the perceived gap between the Europeans and the
alliance leader. Given the enormity of the problems facing
Gorbachev and other Eastern European leaders, quick results
in terms of a rapid expansion of East-West trade can scarcely
be hoped for. There are nevertheless scope and need for bold
and coordinated initiatives by both the Europeans and the
United States.

Conclusions

This chapter has attempted to place the discussion of U.S.–
European relations in a broad, historical, and systemic framework. This is not intended to imply that issues such as reciprocity, access to public procurement, inward investment,
local content, the future of quotas and other special arrangements under Article 115, or the phasing out of subsidies in the
agricultural sector or technological transfers in East-West
trade are unimportant. The maintenance and consolidation of
good relations between the United States and the European
Community—and more generally the development of a new,
peaceful, and constructive relationship with Eastern Europe
and the Soviet Union—will, however, depend on the capacity
of all those involved to agree on their fundamental political
objectives, and their ability to develop a framework for their
discussions and negotiations in which disputes over detail are
subordinated to the overall political goals.

This is particularly true of the West-West relationship. Reference was made earlier to tensions within the Anglo-American alliance in the 1940s. They were by any reckoning very
serious indeed. They were prevented from wrecking the enterprise as a whole, however, because those principally involved,
and in particular the prime minister and the president, never
lost sight of their fundamental community of interest. In the
present context, there is much combustible material on both
sides of the Atlantic. The primary task of the Bush administration, and, it need hardly to be said, of European leaders them-

selves, will be to reaffirm and redefine their community of interests within an institutional framework that points forward to the period after 1992, when the most important subjects will be discussed between the United States and the European Community as such, rather than backwards to an era of asymmetry.

3

U.S.–Japan Economic Relations in the 1990s: A Crossroads?

MICHAEL B. SMITH

I n the early 1990s the United States faces a host of daunting trade and international economic issues. Among these are the nagging American trade deficit, the American response to Europe 1992, and the need for a new debt strategy. But none is more pressing, or seemingly more intractable, than the American relationship with Japan. Neither the United States nor Japan has been able successfully to come to grips with their economic differences. Fundamental issues divide the two economic superpowers, the greatest being the close ties between the Japanese government and its business community as opposed to the almost antibusiness (or, at best, laissez-faire) atti-

MICHAEL B. SMITH is president of SJS Advanced Strategies, a trade and investment consulting firm he established in 1988. From 1979 through 1988, as deputy U.S. trade representative, first in Geneva then in Washington, D.C., he was responsible for multilateral and bilateral trade negotiations, including the Uruguay Round. Ambassador Smith entered the foreign service in 1958 and has a long career of government service with the Department of State and with the White House, ending his thirty years as a career minister in the Foreign Service.

tude of the American government toward its business community.

The American response to growing Japanese economic power has been checkered, at best, and downright suicidal, at worst. Equally, Japanese appreciation of its new-found prowess has been dispersed and self-contradictory as the economic liberalization one would expect from an economic power has been only grudgingly given and leadership only reluctantly assumed. This has led to the gloomy situation in which distrust in economic terms has grown between the two powers. In turn, the U.S.–Japanese relationship increasingly is marked by a rivalry for leadership, rather than a spirit of cooperation to alleviate—if not cure—some pressing global economic problems.

To understand this better, one must first look at the respective economic situations of the two superpowers and the options (or lack of them) these economic facts present each country.

First, with regard to the United States, the international economic picture is bleak. The trade deficit, absent further dollar devaluation or cutting back of domestic consumer spending, will surely worsen and could surpass $200 billion by 1991. The bloom on the export rose is clearly over, and imports, driven by an insatiable consumer mania, will continue to rise. We have not only been transformed from a creditor nation into the world's largest debtor country, but we will most certainly "improve" on that debtor status to over $1 trillion by 1991. The current account deficit is at least as bad as the trade deficit and that, too, will deteriorate much further in the early 1990s. The American savings rate is scandalous, almost the lowest of the countries that belong to the Organization for Economic Cooperation and Development (OECD). Productivity increases are faint and sporadic. The American infrastructure is cracking and creaking, with many unsafe bridges, deteriorating highways, overcrowded airports, and bankrupt transit systems.

Most serious, the American educational system lies in near ruins. We cannot even teach junior high school students to find the United States on a map, let alone how to add or subtract. As former Secretary of Education William Bennett noted, if foreign countries had done to our educational system what we have done ourselves, we would have declared war on those nations. The impact of our substandard educational system on U.S. international competitiveness should be obvious to anyone. Unfortunately, it was not so obvious to the Reagan administration, the U.S. Congress, the media (above all, television), the educators, and the American citizenry.

With regard to Japan, one can see a far brighter international economic picture. Japan's trade surplus grows despite yen appreciation. Japanese business representatives adjusted magnificently to the September 1985 Plaza Accord (which, in essence, allowed for the orderly depreciation of the U.S. dollar) and became more efficient exporters than ever. (U.S. auto manufacturers perversely often did just the reverse—they raised their prices, assuring their continued malaise vis-à-vis their Japanese competitors.) Exports are booming. Japan's saving rate is *six* times higher than the rate in America, and its productivity gains continue to outstrip those in the United States. Its infrastructure is well oiled and greased, with superbly repaired bridges, well-kept highways, new airports, and probably the world's most efficient transit system, although it, too, runs at a financial loss.

More importantly, Japan is educating its students far better than is the United States. In relative terms Japan is producing more engineers, chemists, and other scientists than the United States. In some academic disciplines, the ratio is not relative, it is absolute. Just as America's educational plight holds serious implications for its competitiveness, Japan's superior system portends further economic boom. Its exceptional, growing cadre of educated young promises not only to insure Japan's dominance in trade *but also* America's declining prominence.

Not all is totally rosy in Japan, as will be discussed later, but as we closed out the 1980s, one could conclude that, all other factors being equal, Japan is on the rise and the United States is going downhill. Or, at a very minimum, the United States must get its economic house in order to have *any* chance of enhancing its world influence. The only questions are which, if any, options it will choose.

The bilateral trade deficit between the two powers is too big, everyone says that. The problem is that *no one* does anything about it in a serious, coordinated, consistent way. This leads to distrust between the respective governments of Japan and the United States.

Japan has been a habitual dumper in the U.S. market; everyone knows that. The problem is that *no one* addresses that tendency systematically or coherently. This also leads to distrust by U.S. and Japanese companies alike, not to mention considerable frustration in both governments.

The U.S. government has *always* been a weak supporter of U.S. exporters; everyone knows that. The problem is that *no one* in the government has been able to alter that trend, leading to distrust by U.S. businessmen and accusations of U.S. laziness by the Japanese.

The Japanese government has systematically targeted U.S. industries to dominate; everyone knows that. The problem is that *no one* in power in the United States has been willing to admit that, let alone do anything about it, leading to distrust by frustrated U.S. industries and continuance of the practice by Japan.

U.S. business has increasingly focused on short-term results driven by quarterly stockholder reports; everyone knows that. The problem is that *no one* in the private sector has had the courage to challenge the financiers, so the trade deficit worsens and the distrust rises—in this case through no fault of the Japanese.

Japanese business practices, government tolerated cartels, archaic distribution systems, and culturally approved protectionism all inhibit foreign exports to Japan; everyone knows that. The problem is that *no one* combats these issues directly, either in Japan or overseas, leading to distrust.

The U.S. government has gone to great extremes to protect "rust valley" industries; everyone knows that. The problem is that few have done anything to protect or encourage advanced

U.S. industries' interests vis-à-vis Japan, leading to distrust. Efforts have been undertaken to revitalize industries on behalf of national security interests, e.g., Sematech, but rarely have commercial considerations *alone* been enough to protect or promote an American industry.

These are just a few of the reasons that distrust exists between various parties within the United States and Japan. There are many others. But the fact remains that both U.S. industry and the government are totally frustrated in their attempts to narrow the bilateral trade gap. This frustration is increasingly vented in the Congress (e.g., the 1988 Omnibus Trade and Competitiveness Act), in the business community (e.g., repeated calls for the government to do *something*), and in the government itself (e.g., Market Opening Sector-Specific [MOSS] programs, endless committees, and even more endless studies). Two events in 1989 triggered additional tensions between the United States and Japan: the report of the United States Trade Representative (USTR) to Congress in the spring including Japan on the "Super" 301 list, which cited countries with consistent records of unfair trade practices, and the July Paris Western summit, where U.S. policy on the dollar was seriously criticized by its allies.

Conversely, the Japanese address their frustration with the United States by encouraging "import more" or "import now" programs that do not work, with reports that are only sporadically carried out. Bureaucrats from Japan's Ministry of International Trade and Industry (MITI) have become increasingly antagonistic toward escalating U.S. demands, thus generating further distrust among the two powers. The all too frequent Japanese response has been to agree to U.S. requests for Japan to export less, rather than for Japan to import more.

The frustration factor threatens the relationship between the United States and Japan at a time when they should be moving closer together to true economic cooperation. It is more than a truism that the two superpowers have the ability to lead the world out of much of its poverty and physical ill health. This opportunity, heretofore unique, is in jeopardy because the macro policies of the two have been driven by the micro elements. Paradoxically, the political leaders of both countries have failed to understand the importance in economic terms—let alone political terms—of the micro factors and how they can sour the macro picture.

A classic, if not ludicrous, example of this was the infamous baseball bat case wherein it took the combined efforts of two U.S. cabinet secretaries two years to persuade equally high-level Japanese officials to let U.S.–made aluminum baseball bats into Japan. Imagine, if you can, the U.S. trade representative and the MITI minister sitting across a table from each other arguing about the relative safety of U.S. and Japanese baseball bats, the bats all being identical. The U.S.–Japanese relationship should have ensured that such a petty case was handled routinely and expeditiously at the third secretary level. Instead, the case became a watershed in terms of frustration and one of the great trade comedies of the decade.

At the same time, crucial high-technology industries, such as semiconductors, machine tools, and numerically controlled tools, were facing fierce Japanese competition. Furthermore, U.S. fiber optics and supercomputers were being locked out of Japanese markets. And, while the U.S. political system, in this case the cabinet, fully supported taking action against the Japanese over baseball bats, it refused to address the machine tool problem despite very clear evidence of Japanese government subsidization and targeting of that industry in the United States. Again, a classic case of the micro case (bats) supplanting the macro (machine tools).

Situations like the baseball bat case, which exemplify the era of distrust between the United States and Japan, can be replaced by instances of more equitable exchanges. Together, Japan and the United States can set about building a new era of *true* economic friendship by taking the following steps.

1. Both countries and, more importantly, both governments must stop linking economic and political issues because, inevitably, at least for the United States, this has meant the sacrifice of its economic interests when its political interests were judged of equal value.

2. When the political leaders of these two countries meet,

their entourages should include not only representatives from the Foreign Ministry and State Department, but, also, the spokespersons from economic/commercial/trade ministries. Excluding trade ministers from trade negotiations is the height of folly. Yet this was precisely what happened when President Reagan and Prime Minister Nakasone met in Los Angeles in 1985 to launch the MOSS talks.

3. Greater emphasis should be placed on broader industrial agreements rather than individual items. For instance, the MOSS discussions are designed to provide a bilateral negotiating forum aimed at reducing or removing all government imposed Japanese trade barriers within designated sectors, as opposed to negotiating specific problems on a case-by-case basis.

4. Let bygones be bygones. Government officials from ministers down must now put the past unhappy experiences behind them and move forward on a more mature basis. Reviving the specter of the past may score debating points but does not usually resolve problems.

5. Enhance industry-to-industry cooperation and, particularly, encourage closer liaison between the U.S. Chamber of Commerce, the Keidenren, and their subsets.

6. *Set objectives.* To begin to offset the trade imbalance, the Japanese government and its major industry associations should set import goals for Japan, established as *objectives.* (These objectives should not be legally binding in order to avoid being subject to foreign retaliation if the objectives aren't reached.) Objectives, in the sense of targets to be reached, can serve a useful purpose in focusing on real trade, not just generalities.

7. Abolish all *protectionist* quotas in *both* countries—this means steel, rice, textiles, aluminum, cars, trucks, baseball bats, what have you.

8. Coordinate defense procurement and make the procurement decisions on economic grounds, not—as in the FSX debate—on political grounds. The FSX debate revolves on whether the United States and Japan should jointly produce a

new jet fighter based on the U.S. F-16 plane designed by General Dynamics Corporation. The concept of coproduction is sound; the actual terms of the agreement are flawed. On the plus side, there will be technology transfer both ways; however, more negatively, the transfers will not be balanced, as Japan stands to benefit more under the agreement. Furthermore, the question remains as to why Japan, in this instance, does not buy a U.S. fighter "off the shelf," modified perhaps to particular Japanese requirements.

9. Coordinate defense weapon development and then *share equitably* the ensuing production. For instance, efforts should be made to develop new antisubmarine warfare technology, an area where neither Japan nor the United States possesses adequate means to face the challenge of the "silent" subs.

10. Engage in truly reciprocal research and development projects, where the science and technology advantages are equally shared. This would be particularly beneficial in the area of supercomputers in which both the United States and Japan have invested substantial amounts of money, time, and resources.

11. Open up the financial markets of both countries to each other without reservations.

Now, some of the above thoughts may suggest a U.S.–Japan free trade agreement. Nothing could be further from the truth. It would be a disaster to have such an agreement between the two economic superpowers, for it would signal the beginning of the end to the multilateral trading system. Simply put, it would limit opportunities to bring multilateral pressure on Japan by confining recourse to bilateral terms. Such an agreement would also lead to instant distrust of *both* countries by their Pacific neighbors, to say nothing of the European Community.

All of the above measures are micro oriented in nature but are not minuscule in importance. The financial, defense, and trade elements are irritants, each significant in themselves but only part of a bigger problem.

The bigger problem is the definition—mutually agreed on,

of course—of the economic role each country will or should play in the 1990s and what each country is willing to tolerate. This is the real "macro" side of the equation, which should truly be driving the micro side—"top down" rather than "bottom up."

The first thing Japan and the United States must agree on, perhaps at an economic summit between President George Bush and Prime Minister Toshiki Kaifu, is *not* to dominate the other. The United States, as the military leader of the free world, cannot possibly agree to Japanese economic domination of the Pacific Rim, while the United States spends billions to protect the Rim, including Japan. Likewise, Japan cannot agree to a continuation of the current situation wherein the United States always has a veto in multilateral financial forums even when Japan is the main contributor. Japan should insist on being treated as an equal, because economically it is an equal.

But neither power can afford to be dominated by the other. Each must forswear government sponsored targeting of the other's market. Each leader must forswear subsidies. Each country must forswear dumping. The sharing of power means playing by the same rules *even if* the governmental culture and systems are different. Distrust will turn into trust only when both sides feel both are playing on a "level playing field" from a common rulebook.

Both sides must agree that the Pacific—let alone each other's markets—is not a Japanese or an American pond. Rather, the Pacific is a "common" market, to be peacefully exploited by both. The growing fear in the United States that Japan has monopolistic designs in the region can only be alleviated by more modest Japanese economic activity in the area.

Second, Japan and the United States must reach some understanding on the defense share that each must carry in the Pacific, because national security expenditures divert economic resources from the country's general economy. Japan must spend more, certainly double its current 1 percent of gross national product (GNP), and the United States less—much the same as in Europe. America simply cannot afford any longer to be the defense "bankroller" for the free world. Japan's defense budget of $29 billion may be the free world's third largest, but it is still less than 10 percent of the American defense budget, and Japan's GNP is 50 percent of the U.S. figure. The U.S. defense budget has its economic cost in terms of adding to our federal deficit and depriving the private sector of needed capital. Japan has not faced this problem yet, but it must or the United States must reduce its Pacific share.

Defense burden sharing is not just a political issue. Unfortunately, the United States has never understood this, as the political officers of the State and Defense Departments have always insisted that defense is done for political reasons. Nothing could be more short-sighted, as the United States must defend its economic system as well. The economics of defense are as important as—if not more than—the politics of defense.

As a result, the United States has unconsciously ceded one economic advantage after another to Japan, or assumed one defense cost burden after another without regard to whether Japan could or should pay instead. We are not living in the fifties when only the United States could afford to defend the free world.

The time has come—indeed is overdue—for defense decisions to be undertaken jointly by the political/military *and* the economic/commercial branches of the U.S. government. The secretaries of commerce and treasury have as much right to participate in defense decisions as does the secretary of state—maybe more, as they are responsible for the nation's economic well-being, its jobs, industry, and trade. The Department of State has no such national constituency.

The third area for agreement, and obviously related to the first two, is the role the United States and Japan will play in multilateral affairs, above and beyond the Pacific. By this I mean how leadership can be shared in the numerous multilateral economic forums such as the General Agreement on Tariffs and Trade; the World Bank and the International Monetary Fund; the development banks of Africa, Asia, and Latin America; and the various economic agencies of the United Nations. Japan still does not play a role in these organizations and institutions commensurate with its economic strength, partly because it has not wanted to and partly because the United States, in conjunction with the Europeans, would not let Japan do so. This must change.

More delicately, an understanding must be reached within the Pacific Rim. While Japan may indeed be on an economic roll, its Asian neighbors do not want to be steamrolled by Japan, for obvious historic reasons. But Japan's economic power cannot be denied nor can its legitimate aspirations (indeed, its obligations) to play a greater international role be disaffirmed. Currently, U.S. power to influence and control Pacific economic factors is at its lowest since World War II. At the same time, the economic consequences of democratization in the Pacific are far greater than the political consequences, because with democratization in the Pacific has come market deregulation, market liberalization, and an outbreak of Pacific entrepreneurship. The continuing political democratization in the region depends on continued economic freedom and growth there, and both Japan and the United States must work to foster that economic autonomy, not to control or manage it. In short, both superpowers must agree to let the other Asian countries develop indigenously and not become mere economic satraps, colonies, or outlying branches. Both Japan and the United States must welcome the development of local competitive industries in other Asian/Pacific Rim nations, encourage their exports, and increase technology transfers. For both the superpowers, overseas economic growth lies in a strong Pacific Rim in which neither dominates and both cooperate in a benign fashion.

Hence, as Japan and the United States open the decade of the 1990s, serious consideration should be given by both to the development of a Pacific Rim economic arrangement where the wealth of both economic powers is harnessed to promote a long-term agreement with the other Pacific Rim countries on trade, finance, development, education, and security. Such an undertaking has numerous advantages and few pitfalls.

Such a project would tend to subsume the heretofore constant bilateral bickering beneath an objective larger than the two superpowers. Because economic sacrifices (call them concessions) would have to be made to the other Asian countries, and because some of these sacrifices are also the subjects of bilateral friction (rice, textiles, steel, etc.), some bilateral barriers would disappear as part of the mutual concessions to the Rim by the superpowers.

Also, an arrangement designed to enhance market oriented economies elsewhere in the Rim can only strengthen the market forces within the superpowers themselves. This, in turn, becomes an effective defense against parochial protectionism and a spur to do necessary—and often overdue—internal adjustments. Rice in Japan and textiles in the United States offer classic examples of where overdue internal adjustments could be effected as part of the Rim arrangements.

Next, a Rim accord would help boost the Rim countries in such new areas as services. With acknowledged American and Japanese expertise in the services sector, Asian countries that trail the superpowers in services can only stand to benefit from closer, more formal agreements including technology transfer.

Furthermore, a strong Pacific Rim will act as an effective counterweight to the post–1992 Europe. If, as some fear and suspect, Europe moves toward a "fortress" posture, then both Japan and the United States would have the security of a huge market in the Pacific—as would the other Pacific countries. If the 1992 exercise in Europe turns out to be truly market liberalizing, then the Rim countries have superb opportunities to expand significantly their trade elsewhere in the world, thereby reducing their dependency on each others' markets.

An economic arrangement between Rim countries presumably means that defense levies can be reduced, at least for the United States. Stronger economies in the region not only mean greater political stability but also ensure that the other

Asian countries will ultimately assume an increasing share of the common defense burden now largely carried by the United States.

Also, a forward-reaching Rim arrangement can serve to inspire other areas of the world toward seeking greater economic cooperation. Much has been written recently (mostly negatively) about the growing trend toward regionalism as if the dawn of protectionism were upon us. Actually, regionalism, if liberally oriented, can be tremendously helpful in creating a better economic world.

The United States is, of course, the premier example of successful liberalism and is still the envy of the economic world. And who can argue against the development of the European Common Market, another more recent example of regionalism. Trading blocs are counterproductive only when they are deliberalizing, restrictive, or protective as were some of the Latin American attempts of the 1950s, 1960s, and 1970s.

In fact, Latin America could learn a great deal from the European experience or even that of the Association of Southeast Asian Nations (ASEAN). A Rim arrangement can do even more than ASEAN and almost certainly make other geographic areas around the world look to see how they, too, could cooperate more closely.

Finally, a Pacific Rim economic arrangement can only help subregional disputes or tensions resolve themselves, or speed the process to closer political and economic cooperation. The Korean situation is an example of the latter, and the ASEAN/ Kampuchean tensions are examples of the former. The drive toward a Rim arrangement will itself help regional differences dissipate as the individual partners submerge their own parochial interests before the common "good."

In speaking of grandiose schemes such as the Pacific Rim economic arrangement, one must remain mindful of the real cultural, sociological, and ethnic differences among Pacific Rim nations. Koreans are not Australians, nor Mexicans Singaporeans. The varying levels of economic development in some twenty-odd Rim countries make "balancing" of benefits and obligations very difficult. The geographic distances involved would, in a nonelectronic age, be insurmountable and are still very real despite satellites. But doubters do not build bridges, and naysayers can always be found.

What President Bush and Prime Minister Kaifu have is an opportunity to leave a mark on the world's economic history. President Reagan and Canadian Prime Minister Brian Mulroney did just that, as they reached out and dared to do something really bold and important—the U.S.–Canada Free Trade Agreement.

Bush and Kaifu can do something equally bold, if not greater—the formal launch of a Pacific Rim economic arrangement. Such an accord would involve a series of arrangements, fairly loosely structured, in which the two superpowers undertake economic commitments favoring the other less developed Rim countries (in this they would be joined by Australia, New Zealand, Canada, and possibly Singapore) in trade, finance, and science and technology, or education. All trade barriers (real and hidden) would be reduced or eliminated within the Rim; on finance, debt problems of debtor Rim countries would be handled within the Rim, and all aid projects would be coordinated; on science and technology or education, massive new exchanges of students and transfers of technology would be facilitated.

In return, the other Rim nations would undertake scheduled and programed market liberalization steps. Import substitution policies would be junked, domestic content rules eased, and development requests and projects coordinated. Not every Pacific Rim country needs its own steel mill, nor does every nation need to build supercomputers. Tariffs of nondeveloped Rim countries would first be harmonized to the lowest current figure and subsequently reduced or eliminated. The pace of liberalization would be negotiated for each Rim country and would be binding once agreed upon.

Similar agreements would be negotiated in education, cultural exchange, medical and health services, vocational training, and the like. The overarching intent of all these accords

would be to link the Pacific Rim countries more closely together and thereby derive greater economic benefits for all.
The preferences each would accord to the others would be
exclusively reserved for Rim countries, hopefully sending a
strong signal to non-Pacific countries that economic liberalization will be for the Pacific the wave of the future.

Thus the political leaders of both Japan and the United
States would be advised to channel their search for a bilateral
solution to the trade problem into a joint effort on behalf of a
vigorous, dynamic Pacific Rim agreement. Concentrating
solely or even mainly on the bilateral problems between the
two superpowers will inevitably *and* continually lead to friction, tensions, and nationalistic outbursts. What is needed
is an issue or forum to channel all the bilateral effort on behalf of a greater, better cause. That cause is clearly the Pacific
Rim.

If the Pacific Rim becomes the cause around which the two
superpowers can rally, it still remains for the United States and
Japan to get their domestic economic houses in order, especially in the case of the United States. Foremost of the problems for the United States is, of course, the federal budget
deficit. Unless and until that deficit is brought under control
and reversed, the United States will not be able to play a truly
constructive role in fashioning the Rim arrangement(s). The
Bush administration has extended an olive branch, and possibly passed the buck, to the Congress in the hope that the two
arms of government can reach an understanding on the budget. However important such an understanding may be domestically, it is doubly important internationally. The budget
deficit's greatest long-term damage to the economy is the limi-
tation it places on available savings for private investment. It is
the availability of savings (and hence investment) that ultimately will decide the economic fate of the United States, not
the deficit per se. If the budget continues to drain potential
savings from the economy, private investment will inevitably
decline, making the United States even less competitive in the
future. Hence, from at least the international competitiveness

standpoint, it is in the U.S. interest quickly to reduce that deficit so as to free up capital for investment in new plant and equipment. Again, from the international viewpoint, budget deficits are not morally or ethically evil. Rather, deficits ultimately deprive a country of its ability to be competitive. It is not just a question of inventing a better mousetrap—producing the mousetrap is equally important, and without investment capital available, the mousetrap does not get produced for export. For instance, it is frightening to note how little the Reagan administration understood about the linkages between the deficit, U.S. productive capability, and the nation's ability to compete overseas. The United States is just beginning to pay for its failure to come to grips with this vital equation, and it will feel the repercussions long into the future.

For the Japanese, getting their part of the economic house in order means attacking the land use/rice equation. While the rice import barrier is bothersome to foreigners, like Thailand and the United States, who might like to export rice to Japan, the real losers in this are, of course, Japan itself and its consumers. If Japan wants to spend $20 billion per year to subsidize domestic rice production, that is its sovereign right. It also means Japan has $20 billion less to invest in more profitable areas—also a sovereign right.

But the $20 billion annual subsidy outlay has far greater costs involved. Preserving valuable land for rice production makes other land values even higher and farther out of reach for the average Japanese consumer/home owner. For instance, Tokyo's land prices have tripled over the last four years, reflecting the artificially induced scarcity of land available for development in Japan. Those who own land have no need to save due to the nominal book value of their individual wealth. Furthermore, those who do not own a house have no reason to save since they will never be able to afford one anyway.

This powderkeg situation is of concern to the United States as well as Japan, given substantial Japanese investment in this country. The dollar's continued decline only fuels Japanese investment further. Japan must act before its stock market collapses. The quickest way to bring down land values to more human scales is to let in rice imports and, thereby, drive the high cost and/or inefficient Japanese rice farmer off the land. Painful as this may be—politically above all—it is the only way democratization of land can be accomplished and the aspirations of the young of Japan satisfied. Like tax increases in the United States, land and rice reform measures are politically sensitive subjects in Japan. Just as taxes should be increased in the United States (and will be), so too should rice production be decreased in Japan so that the fixed quantity of land can be redistributed for the greatest economic and social good.

These two actions alone—on the U.S. side, getting the budget under control, and on the Japanese side, addressing the land/rice equation—could do more to restore bilateral harmony and create a favorable atmosphere for real Pacific Rim cooperation than any other measures. For it must not be forgotten that the American competitiveness problem does not involve just the Japanese; our waning competitiveness concerns all of Asia, as Asia depends on an open American market and would suffer traumatically if American protectionism really took hold. Likewise, the Japanese attitude regarding rice imports creates an aura of distrust throughout Asia, which, like Japan, considers rice in an almost mystical context and yet trades far more liberally in this commodity than does Japan. The rice "problem" is not a U.S./Japan problem. Indeed, American industry should perhaps deviously encourage Japan to continue subsidizing rice production. Rather, the rice problem is first a domestic concern in Japan, and second, a problem for Japan within the Rim.

Whether the notion of the Pacific Rim economic arrangement develops or evolves is, in the end, dependent upon the leadership and statesmanship of the two superpowers. Their willingness to bury the hatchet, to forswear nationalistic and mercantilistic interests, and to share both the costs and exhilaration of leadership is, at this point in time, questionable as the bilateral tensions remain extremely strong.

Both Japan and the United States are at a crossroads in their economic relations, not just between themselves but, equally, between themselves and their Pacific neighbors. Being at a crossroads means that there are at least three options ahead, and more negatively, one regressive path behind. Also, being at a crossroads means that one has traveled a certain distance along one road with potentially new, different paths to be taken.

This crossroads analogy is important for the United States and Japan in 1989, as the two superpowers have recently shared a bumpy road, to say the least. The American Congress is unlikely to allow the Bush administration to continue previous economic policies vis-à-vis Japan, i.e., letting the political considerations of the relationship overpower the economic factors and interests. Ninety percent of the reason we have the 1988 Trade Act with its protectionist overtones is because of previous administrations' unwillingness to "take on" the Japanese when it was possible to do so easily. Hence, the Bush administration's room to maneuver with Japan is severely constricted by the Trade Act itself and/or the vigilance of the Congress. More importantly, the leverage the Bush administration enjoys is far less than it could have been because of unilateral economic concessions given to Japan under the guise of collective security (e.g., machine tools, FSX fighter, the F-15 engine, etc.) and the heretofore one-sided approach of the State Department on things Japanese.

Hence, at the crossroads of the 1990s, the United States must take into account the *weakened* American economy, the economic *parity* of America and Japan, and a *resurgent* Japan. Hence, *diverting* the bilateral "contest" into a regional campaign has to be in the U.S. interests. The Pacific Rim gamble for the United States is somewhat of a strategic measure, to channel Japan's economic juggernaut away from mercantilistic ends and into more noble (and, incidentally, less threatening to America) activities for the Rim countries.

Thus the road the United States follows in the 1990s cannot be the same one it has traveled down in the 1980s. The American relationship with Japan in the 1980s has served largely Japanese interests; the Japanese economic assault on the American market has succeeded beyond the wildest dreams (or fears) of anyone, matched only as a mirror reflection by the paucity of the American success in Japan's markets.

Equally, the road Japan has been following cannot be the same in the 1990s. The export oriented growth that Japan enjoyed in the 1970s and 1980s will have to be adjusted as other nations demand a greater share of Japan's market. The grudging trade concessions Japan made, and only in the last half of the 1980s, are but a "down payment" for Japan in the Rim context, to say nothing of the Uruguay Round negotiations. Both the Japanese body politic and the Japanese industries that still receive endless government favors and protection will have to face the real prospect that liberalization pressures will emanate not only from America but from fellow Asians. The pressures will not just involve tariffs and quotas, but the more subtle issues of "depression cartels," "sister" firms and suppliers, the distribution system, and the other tools "Japan, Inc." has used to keep low-cost imports from Japanese shores.

For Japan, the crossroads options offer a new opportunity to exercise regional and indeed global economic leadership. Japan has legitimate aspirations to play a global role in international economics, and such aspirations should be welcomed not only by the United States but, also, by the other nations of the Pacific Rim. The trick will be to "direct" these aspirations in a way benefiting everyone, not just Japanese commercial interests.

In sum, therefore, what new road the United States and Japan each embark upon should be the same road where purely nationalistic objectives are subsumed by a greater objective: the growth and stability of the Pacific economies. This marriage between a common geographic region and compatible economies, coupled with an economic tide of market oriented philosophies and political democratization, provides a chance for the two superpowers to put aside and deflect their perennial micro oriented infighting, and use their human, capital, and technological resources to make the twenty-first century truly the era of the Pacific. The opportunity is present now. It only remains for these two great economic giants to seize that opportunity, exercise the necessary leadership, and become the critical catalysts.

4

Technology and the Economy

HARALD B. MALMGREN

I n virtually every nation there is a sense of urgency about how to improve competitiveness. In policy debate, the role of technology has become a focal point throughout the world. Many policies are being proposed to stimulate innovation, with the aim of boosting national competitiveness.

Long accustomed to maintaining world technological leadership, the United States itself has in recent years entered a period of self-doubt and insecurity about an apparent decline in its international competitiveness and even about its ability

HARALD B. MALMGREN heads Malmgren, Inc. and is director of Malmgren, Golt, Kingston & Company, Ltd., firms that provide business planning and financial advisory services to international corporations and financial institutions. In the 1960s and 1970s, Dr. Malmgren served under three presidents in various official capacities in the office of the U.S. Trade Representative, and was a trade advisor to the Senate Finance Committee. He was also associated with the Defense Department in the early 1960s and, in recent years, has been a frequent advisor to the White House and to various presidential commissions. Dr. Malmgren is the author of many articles and books on international trade, finance, public policy, and business management.

to maintain leadership. Numerous reports of government advisory bodies and of private organizations have been generated in the last decade or so concerning the perceived flagging of the U.S. economy and its ostensible causes. Among the many themes of these reports is a common thread of anxiety about the future of U.S.–generated technology. Many of the policy proposals of these reports are aimed at protecting national industries from "unfair" or "excessive" foreign competition, in order to encourage development of new, home-based technologies.

However, in spite of the universal interest in the role of technology, there is in public policy discussion very little analysis of the real impact of technological change on the world economy. There seems to be a growing perception of a need to encourage structural changes to adapt to the fast changes in the nature of global economic competition. Yet there is little recognition of the revolutionary character of emerging technologies and their potentially overpowering effects on governments and their national economic policies.

Technology is now evolving more rapidly and more pervasively than at any time in human history. The pace and scope of change are so powerful that historic discontinuities are becoming visible in economic, political, and social structures, and perhaps even in the global environment and in the characteristics of life forms that inhabit our world.

It is my view that we need to take an entirely new perspective about what is happening, that the rapid transformation of our economies can best be understood within the context of a new historic paradigm. Technological advances now well under way, and cost advantages of their applications, are giving rise to major structural adjustments in all national economies, and are causing substantial shifts in the pattern of world movement of goods, services, and capital.

Technological advances are bringing about profound changes in the organization of work, of governance, and of social life. The economic and social disruptions that inevitably characterize rapid change are challenging governments, as their citizens call for action to offset or ease the pains of adjustments. However, these advances are moving faster than the ability of governments to address and cope with their consequences. Traditional powers of national governments are being rapidly eroded by the internationalization, or globalization, of change.

Major Technological Thrusts

There are many ways in which to categorize or conceptualize the major thrusts of technological change that are now at work.

The Information Revolution

One of the most powerful technological forces of recent years has been the acceleration of advances in the generation, gathering, transmission, and processing of information through advances in microelectronics and in measurement.

The accelerated pace of progress in integrated circuits is now becoming widely understood, with cost per function decreasing by a factor of two while doubling in complexity every year for more than two decades. This technology of compression or miniaturization is still not approaching any clear limits, and it is generally expected that densities of active components will continue to increase for the foreseeable future.

Integrated circuit technology is the best known element of the information revolution, but it is not the only source of dynamism. Developments in photonics and in transmission of information through fiber-optic systems have vastly expanded the transmission capacity of all information systems while reducing "noise" and drastically reducing cost per unit of information.

Rapid advances in semiconductor technology combined with digital electronics are enabling similar advances in computer technology. These advances are driven by a continuous interaction or feedback between microprocessor advances and computer assisted design (CAD) advances. These advances are further strengthened by developments in materials, and in the manipulation of materials through increasingly fine measurement and advances in such areas as electron beam technology.

Software continues to be a more significant constraint on progress than physical or natural limits, but software is nonetheless progressing sufficiently rapidly that we can foresee rapid advances in human-machine interaction that will generate a strong feedback process, giving further impetus to computer advances.

In essence, the convergence of many technologies is providing enormous economies of scale in the accumulation and use of information. This in turn provides enormous economies of scale in supplying services and in transferring technology.

The changes taking place in information management are so far-reaching that some scientists have characterized the changes as constituting "the Information Revolution," in historic terms comparable to or even greater than the changes that took place during the Industrial Revolution.

The consequences of more powerful memories and declining costs of information processing have already begun to transform global modes of communication and the structure of the telecommunications industry itself. That is visible to most people. But this represents only a small part of the revolution.

Scientific research and applied, commercial research are being accelerated as past knowledge is made more readily available and experimentation is assisted by simulation and the interaction of people and computers. There is also an acceleration of innovation, as scientists and engineers find it increasingly possible to draw together developments in many different fields to synthesize incrementally new concepts that typically constitute significant innovations.

The Emergence of New Materials

There has been a fundamental reversal in the direction of technological change in materials science. Historically, technology has been used to process materials found in the earth or growing upon it. From the earliest moments of human life to this century there have been developments one after another in the use of natural resources, to the point where most of our industries and key elements of our economy are resource based.

However, recent advances in materials science and engineering are making it possible "to start with a need and then develop a material to meet it, atom by atom" (as noted by J.P. Clark and M.C. Fleming in *Scientific American,* October 1986). These advances are sometimes now being publicly characterized as constituting a "materials revolution."

During this historic swing from the processing of resources to the creation of new materials there have emerged many hybrid materials, or human-made materials, partly dependent upon traditional resources and processes and partly dependent upon entirely new materials structures.

Among the many new materials are some familiar to the public, such as carbon fiber composites used in tennis rackets and fishing rods—but also used in the manufacture of structural parts of aircraft and other roles of substitution for steel and aluminum. Such new composites are generated by traditional textile fiber companies, and are opening entirely new avenues of business expansion for companies once thought to be on the death list writ by economic change. Another example is the emergence of fine ceramics, widely thought to be useful in home articles such as scissors and cookware, but far more potentially significant in extreme temperature applications such as high-performance, high-heat engines, packaging of integrated circuits and various types of sensors, and containment of space vehicle systems.

The new materials are appearing in many other forms, such as optical fibers, superpolymers, and superconductors. A common aspect of the many new materials is that they are often substitutes for traditional materials derived from both renewable and nonrenewable natural resources. In other words, optical fibers are a substitute for copper in telecommunications applications; ceramics, composites, and superpolymers are substitutes for ferrous and nonferrous metals generally.

We are in a period of economic history where the world's production capacity for ferrous and nonferrous metals well exceeds world demand. There are many reasons for overbuilding, mainly related to the policies of support for such industries in many nations. Over the next decade or two the emergence of new materials produced in growing volume with declining relative cost will generate a powerful new force of competition for existing metals industries, and bring into question the viability of many traditional or older enterprises and production facilities.

In other words, the materials revolution is transforming the fundamental landscape of our industrial structure, bringing into question many of our traditional perspectives on the criticality of particular materials or particular enterprises and industries.

The popular arguments about the potential "deindustrialization" of America, focused on traditional basic industries like steel, have scarcely touched upon this reality, that entirely new industries are emerging, and that old enterprises in one sector are being transformed into new enterprises competing in entirely different sectors. The restructuring of traditional market segments and traditional modalities of competition cuts across all national economies, making meaningless many of our old ideas about how best to manage and encourage market competition.

The Industrial Manufacturing Revolution

The information revolution and materials revolution together are opening the way for fundamental changes in how our enterprises and even our economies function. Industrial processes are being reoriented within the framework of computer assisted design, computer assisted manufacturing (CAM), computer integrated manufacturing (CIM), and other concepts such as flexible manufacturing systems (FMS).

This is not simply a question of "automation," or replacement of labor with machines. The emerging reorientation of industrial processes is based upon multipurpose, reprogrammable equipment and systems, combined with entirely new materials processing techniques. The changing character of production processes provides opportunity for much greater flexibility, through small lot production on large-scale integrated systems, through reduction of inventory requirements by tailoring production to specific demands in very quick response, through accelerated responses to changing demand, while maintaining and even enhancing economies of scale in the use of plant and equipment.

The greater reliance on CIM, and the improvements in production systems that become possible with CIM (such as robotics, automated transfer, laser processing, and new techniques for precision forming and shaping) will tend to reduce the significance of labor costs in competitiveness. This labor-displacing effect in manufacturing will no doubt have significant implications for the competitiveness of enterprises in plants, and even nations that rely on low labor costs for international competitiveness. (For example, automation of sewing and new processes of bonding fabrics will greatly alter the world pattern of apparel production and trade—with enormous consequences for labor use in many geographic locations where apparel manufacture is the single most important employer.)

But the implications for the role of labor are not the most important consideration. Rather, the most significant effect of the transformation of industrial activity is the ability to adjust products continuously, tailoring them to continuously changing requirements of individual users. The flexibility and agility of the new industrial processes allow a much closer interaction between user and producer. It allows, and even requires, producers to work directly with users in the design and application of products, interweaving engineering and other services with the provision of hard goods.

What this means, in essence, is that modern industry will be able to come back full circle to its beginnings in the last century, when individual suppliers and cottage industries produced one-off, one-of-a-kind consumer goods like suits, or producer goods like single-purpose machinery. In other words, the long experience of producing standardized items for off-the-shelf sale may be coming into a period of decreasing relevance, while provision of tailored or specially designed products may be an entirely new mode of competition, based upon large-scale systems that are highly flexible. Such a transformation would also tend to shorten or compress product life cycles, giving the competitive edge to the suppliers with the fastest response time rather than to those with the cheapest off-the-shelf, standardized items.

In the context of the new industrial revolution, competitiveness will increasingly depend upon speed of response and character of product related services.

The Transportation Revolution

These profound developments are being even further enhanced by a number of other technological forces. One of the most significant of these can be found in acceleration of improvements in transportation, especially in aerospace technology, bringing production centers and markets much closer in terms of time and relative cost.

These advances are derived from the powerful convergence of the three thrusts already noted, the information revolution, the materials revolution, and the industrial manufacturing revolution. Yet the momentum behind these advances has also derived from a new process of innovation through systems engineering—the synthesizing of new concepts from a wide variety of separate, highly specialized technical disciplines.

The significance of these developments in movement of people and goods, especially through various segments of air and space, should not be underestimated. Lighter but stronger airframes and lighter, higher-performance aircraft engines will mean greater weight capacity, greater distance feasibility, and shorter landing and takeoff requirements, thereby intensifying the competitiveness of air transport relative to other modes of transportation. New modes of space flight such as the "hyperplane" or "Orient Express" will open even more widely the options. The competitive pressures in transportation will inevitably give even greater emphasis to speed of response in meeting the changing requirements of consumers or users.

The Openings from Biotechnology

A somewhat different convergence of technological advances has opened the way for profound breakthroughs in research in the functioning of living organisms. We are now entering an era in which the alteration of life forms is possible through human-made adjustments in the most fundamental codes of nature.

It is already widely recognized that agricultural applications of some of the new scientific ideas promise to alter the outlook for food production and the nature of agribusiness globally. But the rapid advances are not limited to the provision of food and feed. The new technologies are opening the way to major advances in such diverse areas as industrial processing of materials, the management of wastes, and the functioning of computers.

But beyond these many specific applications is the likelihood that animal and human characteristics will become subject to conscious alteration. Among the foreseeable prospects are that memory will be improved, the functioning of the human at older age levels will be improved, dysfunctional behavior will become subject to physiological correction, and the defense systems of life forms will be strengthened. Unfortunately, it is also possible that unforeseen dangers will be generated by life-altering technologies.

In essence, technological advances are not only opening new avenues of productive activity, but, potentially, new avenues of evolution. It is difficult to visualize a more dramatic example of historic discontinuity than the new-found ability to alter life forms. As these technological advances continue, the life sciences will inevitably move from their past damage-limiting role to a far more central role in the management of our lives, our economies, our social structures, our ecosystem.

The most fundamental effects of these technological advances probably lie somewhat further out in time than the effects of the major thrusts already elaborated. But they promise to give even further impetus to the rapid technological changes that are already unfolding, and will continue to unfold in coming decades.

The Compression of Time

Technological change has been under way since the beginnings of human life. Throughout history, technological change has been altering the patterns of world economic activity. What is different now is that the pace of change has been accelerated, and the modalities of change have moved from adaptation of what exists in nature to conscious changes in the character of nature's building blocks.

A major impact of the information revolution is that it provides opportunities for acceleration of all forms of research and innovation—making available past knowledge, present avenues of inquiry, and simulated future developments all at once, and all together, covering virtually every technical field that might conceivably be relevant.

But this is not just a matter of stepping up the pace of basic research. It also means acceleration of innovation. Innovation in recent decades has mainly derived from incremental changes in the way we do things, usually inspired by synthesizing knowledge and investigation in a variety of related technical fields and management disciplines. The newly emerging technologies are opening the way for accelerated review of the options, drawing upon knowledge and inquiries throughout the world at any given moment in time. A breakthrough in one geographic location is often made available at virtually any other location within a very short time period—not only by drawing upon published results, but also through continuous "online" interaction of thinkers and researchers through direct communication on a global basis.

The use of information is also being enhanced and accelerated. This means that the quality of information available in making economic decisions is improving rapidly. It also means that the time taken to gather and assimilate information is being compressed drastically.

The economic behavior patterns that presently characterize the world economy of today, and that are embodied in institutional and political processes of decision making, are very time-sensitive. Time is taken to evaluate new ideas and assess their commercial potential. Producers seek, and plan on, adequate time to ensure that expected returns can be achieved from slow-gestation plant and equipment investments that implement new technologies. Competitive countermeasures take time to develop and to put in motion.

More rapid technological and economic changes invariably mean disruptions to specific sectors, geographic regions, and groups of people. These disruptions usually result in political pressures to alleviate the pains of adjustment or retard its pace. It takes time to respond to and deal with petitions for government assistance or action to shield specific groups from the disruptive effects of change or of intensified competition. Legislative or even regulatory changes take a long time to develop. And when one government must deal with another government in negotiations on resolving salient problems, the outcome often takes years to shape.

When solutions are devised, there are congenital tendencies in our economic institutions and political processes to try to slow things down, to seek breathing time, and to retard the pace of structural change through measures aimed at shielding disrupted interest groups from the global forces of change. Thus we can see strong counterforces at work: the ability of economic decision makers to act far more rapidly, and the efforts of large institutions and governments to slow down the pace of change.

The cybernetic processes of government as we know it are too slow to cope with the pace of technological change. More decentralized, more timely decisions taken by business enterprises are rapidly reshaping our economic and social structure, and even our ecosystem. These enterprises are increasingly internationalized, with the ability to draw financial support from the agnostic global capital market, which has no national loyalties, and with the ability to shift production bases from one location to another as economic and political circumstances change.

Some social scientists have recently been pointing to emerging tensions between the new global "corporatism" and national governments. These growing tensions are symptomatic of the fundamental changes taking place in how daily decisions are being made in our world economic system, based upon the faster response times of business enterprises relative to governments. This gradual shift of the center of gravity of economic decision making toward corporate enterprises has been facilitated by the widening reliance of governments on market oriented policies and on universal efforts to regulate and liberalize the relations of government and economic enterprises—even in the centrally planned economies.

Timeliness and Competitiveness

Enterprises themselves are undergoing rapid change as well, as their operational focus shifts from competition in the sale of a standard product that embodies a specific array of technologies to competition in the provision of new technologies that meet the specific requirements of particular users. This reorientation is most notable in the restructuring of manufacturing industry, which is described in the discussion of the industrial manufacturing revolution above.

For many decades, the path to major economies of scale lay in standardization of products and repetition of their production. The new manufacturing technologies maintain many of the benefits of large-scale production while allowing continuous change in the products supplied—and while reducing the relative role of labor in final value of products.

The convergence of material technology, manufacturing technology, and information technology presents an entirely new framework of competitiveness. First, the accelerated pace of technological change and the flexibility of production systems require a fundamentally different way of thinking about product life cycles. In past decades, a decision was made from time to time to consolidate the ongoing flow of technology at a given moment and embody it in a standardized product that was expected to have a viable economic life of several years. It was necessary to hold technology of a given product steady for a lengthy period in order to achieve economies of scale, and so-called learning curve economies.

Today it is possible to utilize a given production system and produce a variety of products tailored to specific user needs at any given moment. The products supplied are continuously changing, utilizing flexible, reprogrammable systems. The continuous flow of technological change need not be arrested to embody it in a product; each new item can embody the newest variation or innovation.

Consequently, product life cycles are being drastically shortened. An end-user or consumer product may be introduced on the basis of an expected "half-life" of only, say, eighteen months. The first six months entail moving down the learning curve and moving out on the curve of economies of scale. The next twelve months provide the profits that cover the high introduction costs of the first six months. Thinking this way, new products must be continuously introduced, one after another, to remain moving out on the production curves. This, for example, is one of the fundamental drives in Japanese semiconductor competition.

Second, flexibility and faster response capabilities enable producers to focus more precisely on individual user needs. This in turn encourages much closer interaction between producer and user. Since "tailoring" of products requires technical expertise in user applications, the traditional reliance on sales personnel must be set aside in favor of the use of technicians and engineers to work with users in an ongoing relationship. Products are increasingly sold in conjunction with services.

This ever closer interaction of producer and user means that both parties increasingly find themselves working on the same problems in a mutually supportive manner, with suppliers helping in the engineering work of users. The automotive parts and components business is increasingly moving in this direction, for example. The emerging market for Application Specific Integrated Circuits (ASIC) is based upon the same kind of producer-user interaction. As provision of services grows in connection with sales of goods, the scope of services tends to widen, to cover many other aspects of the relationship, even finance.

Third, because of the advances in information technology, the speed of delivery of services is accelerating greatly. There are major economies of scale in the collection, transmission, and use of information within the framework of the new technologies. This means faster service delivery at decreasing cost, combined with growing capacity of information systems to accept widening demands.

As it becomes cheaper to deliver services, to remote locations as well as to nearby locations, an old business question returns to the forefront: whether to sell technology and services or whether to embody those technologies and services in the form of hard goods. Increasingly the balance is shifting toward the former in major enterprises in key industrial sectors; for smaller enterprises growth has become possible without converting technology and services into things to be sold.

Within the services sectors as such, technological change is opening radically new avenues for meeting consumer needs—through online telecommunications interaction characterized by rapidly growing capacity and decreasing cost. This phenomenon is already a familiar one in banking and in the provision of design and engineering services; it is becoming a viable new avenue for the provision of medical and health services to people who remain at home, rather than going to hospitals.

Fourth, as the interaction of producer and user intensifies, and as goods and services supplied become more tailored, various traditional organizational functions become decreasingly important: management of inventories, distribution mechanisms, sales personnel, etc. become less central to operations. The ability to interact directly with users, and to understand very current requirements and potential new demands, obviates the need for much "middle management." We can already see this phenomenon at work in the drastic reduction of middle management and sales forces in many large enterprises.

But time compression does not only offer new modalities of competition; it also generates new pressures on enterprises to speed up response times in the face of rapidly changing market circumstances. Competitiveness is increasingly defined in terms of the timeliness of response to changing demand, to changing technological possibilities, to changing strategies of competitors—or more succinctly, to a rapidly, continuously changing market.

The key elements to competitiveness in past decades were standardization and productivity; getting costs down while meeting broad and stable segments of demand was the path to success. The key to competitiveness now involves a combination of high productivity and much faster responses, or timeliness. In the future, the emphasis on speed of response will grow relative to the traditional focus on productivity. Competitiveness tomorrow will be determined by timeliness.

Management of Change

The new technologies permit major changes in the structure of management. The new requirements of competitiveness necessitate fundamental changes in how enterprises or economic activities are managed.

The Industrial Revolution and its emphasis on standardization brought a perceived need for hierarchical management. The military model of top-down, structured decision making became the model for virtually all economic enterprises—and even for the centrally planned economies, which were really just extremely large enterprises.

The convergence of new technologies and the accelerated pace of change are bringing into question the effectiveness of our now familiar top-down hierarchical management models. It has become commonplace to state that innovation and entrepreneurship are more likely to flourish among independent businesspeople and small enterprises. It has become popular

in the analysis of the management of large enterprises to rec-
ommend decentralization and greater autonomy of research
and development (R&D) facilities or greater autonomy for
managers of individual lines of business.

The debate about how to improve management to meet the
new competitive realities seems to me too much confined to
the traditional top-down hierarchical concepts. In a market
environment that requires close producer-user interaction and
a much higher speed of response, the hierarchical model does
not fit very well—much like the twentieth century experiences
of guerrilla, or improvisational, warfare have taught us that
top-down military hierarchies perform badly when immediate
adaptation at the point of contact is required.

In the new technological environment, small enterprises
may often prove more agile. But large enterprises can also
behave in a far more flexible manner if the structure of decision making allows it. The extraordinary successes of Japanese
industrial enterprises in the last two or three decades provide
dramatic evidence that bottom-up improvisation, based upon
teamwork or consensus building, can provide strong economic
momentum without any definitive direction from above.

But this raises a deep and troubling question about the prospects for the American management model: can a social structure based upon the primacy of individualism, and a cultivation of narcissism, generate the fruits of organized activity
without top-down management? Alternatively, can such an in-
dividualistic society adopt new values that would encourage
greater teamwork and a greater emphasis on consensus building in organizing economic activities? And if we were to seek a
different balance between individualism and group orientation, would we lose some of the innovativeness and entrepreneurship generated by our present social structure and
narcissistic value system?

My instinctive response is that adaptation of our values and
our decision structures to provide for greater emphasis on
group activities and bottom-up innovation does not necessarily mean giving up the underlying strength of the American
economy, which has always been its innovative, experimental,

pragmatic approach to solving economic problems and creating new economic opportunities. We have already witnessed in recent years different, less hierarchical management systems introduced in many new production facilities in such diverse sectors as electronics and automotive production. We also have long experience of reliance on teamwork in facing many kinds of crises in our nation, ranging from war to local disasters.

Management in the new technological environment must plan for change, rather than plan to meet fixed perceptions of the marketplace. Planning for change means working on the assumption that the market environment is continuously being transformed and that the economic context is subject to turbulence and sudden changes in direction. Planning for change necessitates developing a decision structure that can respond quickly to changes at the point of contact with individual segments of the marketplace. Such points of contact are at the level of individual lines of business, or at the level of specific producer-user interaction. Top management cannot possibly function effectively in a top-down decision structure in such a market environment.

Similarly, the structured framework within which industrial labor has learned to work since the inception of the Industrial Revolution is now becoming outmoded. Traditional reliance on work rules, job descriptions, and other rigid defenses of labor interests in dealing with top-down management is now proving counterproductive. New industrial facilities require far less direct labor and require far more versatility in the roles of workers. In a new facility there is much less need for welders, painters, assemblers, maintenance workers, etc. and greater need for versatile industrial technicians who can themselves manage the highly flexible capital equipment that constitutes factories of today and of the future.

Structural Implications

In the emerging world market environment we must assume that there will be many shifts in relative competitiveness within and among industrial sectors, and shifts in the structure of competitiveness and the relative economic power of nations.

In the new technological environment, the physical location of production may in some cases be in close proximity to end users, and in other cases be far away. The ability to utilize modern telecommunication and information systems globally allows tailored production at remote locations, and rapid improvements in transportation diminish the relative importance of transportation and distribution costs. On the other hand, the need for much closer producer-user interaction may often dictate the location of production in close proximity to the market.

What is essential to note here is that relative labor costs at alternative locations will tend to be less significant in the determination of the location of production of goods and services. The new industrial technologies clearly result in far lower dependence on labor in production. (The share of direct labor costs in final value will continue to diminish, to levels below 5 percent.)

It was fashionable in the United States in the last decade or two to express worry about the transfer of American industrial plants to foreign locations, or about the growing reliance of U.S. manufacturers on "outsourcing" from foreign suppliers of parts and components. This process was descried as a hollowing out of the U.S. industrial base.

Yet we now see many foreign enterprises starting up new manufacturing operations inside the United States, or acquiring existing facilities inside the United States, with the aim to supply the American market from domestic production systems. It was at one time said that such new foreign owned facilities would simply be screwdriver or assembly operations, and that the major jobs would still be lost to foreigners. But many of the new foreign owned manufacturing facilities now coming into being are aiming at 80 percent U.S. content—a target higher than that met by many existing U.S. manufacturers.

Exchange rate changes in the last three years or so have had something to do with this new phenomenon. But many of the

foreign decisions to establish new production facilities inside
the United States were made before the September 1985 Plaza
meeting and before the late 1985 fall of the dollar. The major
force at work was the industrial manufacturing revolution,
which allowed new approaches to manufacturing with much
less attention to relative labor costs. The weakening of the
dollar has simply accelerated this process, by making the ac-
quisition of assets and the building of new plants in the United
States extraordinarily cheap, compared to prospective costs in
other global geographic locations.

A similar process of transplanting production can now be
seen in the European Community, as large non–EC enterprises are responding to the rapid opening and consolidation
of a single European market.

But this raises many questions about competitiveness and
comparative advantage in all nations. For example, there is
likely to be change in the global demand for labor, but in uncertain ways. Transformation of manufacturing processes,
such as through automation of sewing and bonding in the production of apparel, or the elimination of human assembly operations in many manufacturing activities, will alter the industrial development prospects of many developing nations.
Labor demand in some geographic regions may fall drastically,
while rising dramatically in other geographic regions where
skill levels are high and a technological orientation is easy to
implement.

Industrial and agricultural jobs will continue to shrink as a
share of total employment, even in those cases where present
levels of production are maintained in specific locations. Job
requirements will continue to change, and may vary continuously over the life of particular workers—placing a new emphasis on versatility as compared with learning particular
skills.

In the new technological environment of rapid, continuous
change, education will inevitably become a more central determinant of competitiveness and comparative advantage. An
abundance of unskilled, uneducated workers will be less an

opportunity for new growth and more an impediment to improved economic well-being.

In the new technological environment, the traditional reliance of some nations on natural resources may turn into an economic nightmare. The emergence of new human-made materials and the new industrial process technologies are bringing to bear an entirely new array of competitive pressures on traditional resource producers, adding to the already existing pains of global overcapacity.

The technological transformation of global systems for delivery of services will also greatly change present patterns of competitiveness and comparative advantage. On the one hand, the enormous economies of scale of telecommunications systems will encourage consolidation of a variety of services and their delivery through new, global information networks. On the other hand, small innovative entities can provide services globally through the same kinds of mechanisms, in such varying fields as engineering, software support, medical diagnostics, and management information services. Once supporting services such as software development can be routinized, it will be possible to assign such services activities to remote locations (such as assignment of technical support activities to underemployed technicians in South Asia).

In the rapidly changing global market environment, continuous appearance of new entrants domestically and internationally should be expected, encouraged by the accelerated international diffusion of technology. The new competitors may take many forms, including new competitors in nations that formerly did not compete in such sectors, and old industries that introduce new lines of business based on technologies that cut across their traditional market boundaries (such as the emergence of textile producers as competitors in the production of new composite materials that compete with metals).

Government Policy Responses

As noted earlier, governmental processes of decision making are inherently slow. The technological pace is likely to exceed greatly the ability of governments to address specific industrial difficulties or disruptions.

The recent trend toward deregulation and greater market orientation in economic policies does tend to enhance the effects of technological change, by allowing greater flexibility and resilience among enterprises. This trend also reduces the number of instruments available to government to influence or guide the activities of enterprises. Moreover, national budget strictures preclude liberal use of government subsidies or incentives to assist enterprises.

This trend toward "less government" was led by ideologists of the right, who have long believed in the primacy of market forces. Such conservatives also believe that government should be less active in general, and intervene only in response to complaints. This philosophic approach led the U.S. government in the 1980s to place greater emphasis on dealing with complaints from private business interests, rather than try to anticipate problems. But it is inevitable that a process that is dependent upon complaints from specific interest groups will tend to focus on specific, narrowly defined sector problems that are perceived at a given point in time. The complaints usually relate to problems encountered in the recent past, with evidence submitted based on past experience. Since government responses are inevitably slow, new policies aimed at dealing with complaints about past problems usually miss the objective of dealing with new, evolving difficulties.

Moreover, in the absence of other instruments, there is an inevitable tendency to look to import restrictions as a means of insulating troubled enterprises. The justification usually given is that foreign enterprises and governments are engaged in unfair practices—which usually means different practices from those characteristic of the U.S. economy.

Thus if the practices of other nations vary from those of the

United States, there is a tendency to ascribe the deviation as an "unfair practice," which gave rise to the complaint. The result has been in the 1980s in the U.S. a growing array of import restrictions on specific manufactures.

Such restrictive remedies often have unforeseen consequences. The growth in U.S. and European Community import restrictions (antidumping actions, voluntary export restraint agreements, etc.) in the 1980s encouraged foreign-based manufacturers to relocate their production facilities inside the United States, and therefore inside the protective walls of import restrictions.

In general, it could be said that most efforts of governments to relieve the pains of industrial adjustment end up as policies to slow down the adjustment and reduce external competitive pressures. Most industrial assistance policies have the effect of keeping present management in position—even though it could be argued that the problems of most enterprises are attributable to the failure of management to anticipate the technological and competitive forces at work globally. There are many reasons for this, ranging from the invisibility of the costs of import protection to the popularity of measures that appear to hit foreigners more than domestic interests.

It is also clear in the experience of the United States that government efforts to assist and guide technological change have rarely been effective—some notable exceptions being the building of nuclear weapons, the early successes of NASA, and the many advances promoted by the Department of Agriculture.

In the latter 1980s there developed a new surge of interest in the idea of government assisted and guided technology projects to help U.S. enterprises regain or hold on to technological leadership. Proponents of such government-led projects argue that Japan and other industrialized nations do this successfully. The reality is somewhat different: Japan and other nations did try to do this in the past, but in recent years industrial enterprises have resisted cooperation with each other and with government, in their quest for competitive advantage and freedom of action internationally.

More fundamentally, it is questionable whether slow-moving governments can systemically adapt quickly enough to address the new competitive realities. This skepticism is further enhanced when one recognizes that fast-moving, adaptive, successful enterprises rarely request government assistance. Rather it is the slower enterprises that usually find themselves behind the curve of change, and seek new forms of industry-government cooperation.

Winners rarely ask government for help. It is the losers who come to Washington and other capitals. To set policy in response to the complaints of firms that have already begun to fall behind is to be led by losers.

Sound policy should be anticipative policy, addressing the process and pace of change, rather than specific problems of the recent past. Policies that anticipate the future cannot have a high chance of success if they are aimed at specific economic outcomes. A viable technology might be achieved, but its economic sustainability may be in question because of many parallel developments outside the scope of a government program. Policies that anticipate the future should be directional rather than specific, and aim at facilitating change rather than retarding change.

The first requirement of sound policy is to recognize the dynamics of technological change, and especially to recognize the acceleration of change that characterizes our time in history. In this way of thinking, a key role of government ought to be to educate the public, including business enterprises, about the nature of the forces now at work and the major structural changes that will be necessary to meet them. When political pressures build for intervention in specific parts of the economy, governments should try to illuminate for the public at large the underlying structural problems and the complexity of adjustments to changing global circumstances.

In this connection, it would be useful for the U.S. government, and probably for many other governments as well, to derive lessons from the experience of Japanese industry and government in devising "visions" of future technological and economic thrusts that are likely to shape the pattern of future economic growth. These "visions" are not plans, but rather consensual estimates of the currents of technology and their likely direction in coming years, based upon extensive exchanges of view among government agencies, research institutions, academics, and industrial enterprises. This idea has been recently supported by the Manufacturing Studies Board of the National Research Council, in conjunction with the National Academy of Engineering and the National Academy of Sciences, in an overview of the future of U.S. manufacturing (*Toward a New Era in U.S. Manufacturing: The Need for a National Vision*).

Anticipative policy should address systemic questions. Thus governments should pursue macroeconomic policies and general fiscal policies that encourage faster innovation, investment, and growth. Policies should be aimed at creating an economic environment that favors continuous creation of new enterprises and continuous adaptation of existing institutions and enterprises. Conversely, policies that rely for their implementation on assisting existing enterprises, and on concentrating new technology development in them (as may be the tendency in the European Community and the United States) will tend to aggravate the difficulties of structural adjustment.

Anticipative policy must address the fundamental elements of competitiveness in the new technological environment. Among the most important determinants of competitiveness will be the capabilities of the labor force. The relative need for traditional industrial jobs based on specialized skills will diminish in the industrial workplace of coming years. The need for versatile workers who can be continuously reeducated for new tasks will grow.

Since none of the new technologies can function well without human participation and management, the real question is not about labor displacement but about changing labor requirements. New technologies are driven by innovation at all levels of economic activity, not only in research facilities. Innovative, responsive business enterprises achieve success through innovative, responsive behavior of employees. In other words, workers are participants in the process of adaptation and innovation, rather than performers of fixed functions.

Workers of the future will need an educational foundation that provides flexibility and adaptability in what they can do. At the same time, management structures have to be adapted to the new realities, by giving far greater emphasis to bottom-up decision making and greater freedom of action among the various lines of business and at the various points of market contact. What this really means is that successful management will find it necessary to give a new priority to in-house education and training, on a long-term or even lifetime basis, aiming at continuous upgrading and reorientation of workers. The fixed cost of labor will rise as the direct costs of labor decline; but the new labor force will be far more adaptable, if competitiveness is to be assured.

In the new technological environment, governments will find it increasingly difficult to address problems and opportunities of technological change from a purely nationalistic perspective. The dynamics of the new technological revolution transcend national boundaries, just as they transcend sectoral boundaries and the boundaries of traditional scientific and technical disciplines. Purely national R&D programs are likely to be less and less successful. The name of the game for governments in the future will be transnational, or international, cooperation in those areas of technology that are inadequately addressed by autonomous enterprises and research centers. This includes next-generation technologies and technologies that have global implications, but which are of much less interest to specific enterprises. In the latter category are the global questions facing our ecological system, such as the management of wastes and the greenhouse effect.

Vague thinking about the need for international technological cooperation was initiated at the 1982 Western Economic Summit, but little came of it. The other leaders in the economic summit process want these questions to be addressed in the next summit meeting, but it remains a question whether the United States is ready for such a globally oriented dialogue on a transnational basis.

Global Competitiveness

There can be little doubt that the United States remains at the forefront in developing new technologies. Some other nations are demonstrating an ability to excel in specific technologies, but there is no evidence that whole nations are beginning to overtake the United States in generating technological change.

On the contrary, U.S. universities and research institutions are the main centers of scientific and engineering education for the entire world—with little prospect that this role will change in the near future.

One of the problems in maintaining U.S. competitiveness has been the slowness of American enterprises to adapt or respond to the fast-changing technological environment; whereas Japanese enterprises have demonstrated extraordinary successes in implementing new technologies in their industrial processes. Some of the difference between the two nations may be cultural, in some broad sense of that word, but much of the difference may be attributable to different organization of economic activities and different management mechanisms. Japanese enterprises operating on the basis of bottom-up evaluations and decisions have been more responsive to change and more quick to alter products and processes to changing market needs. U.S. enterprises operating primarily on the basis of slow-moving, top-down decision processes have been slow to change.

The U.S. economy remains a powerful but enormously flexible economy. Its fundamental strengths have not gone away suddenly. Other nations have not suddenly spawned superhumans and superscientists who have flown over the heads of U.S. managers and leaders. The reality is that humans do not fly.

U.S. competitiveness in the future will depend upon

whether we can speed up the process of economic change, and speed up the adaptation of our enterprises to the new market realities.

Similarly, competitiveness of enterprises and economic sectors in every nation will increasingly depend upon flexibility, adaptability, and responsiveness to changing market requirements and rapidly changing technological opportunities. Making the same thing every day, cheaply, will not provide a sound basis for maintaining competitiveness.

Competitiveness is timeliness in coming years. If enterprises are to be competitive, they must be managed in such a way that rapid adaptation becomes a way of life at every level of enterprise activity. What this really means is a change in how enterprises operate, with far less emphasis on hierarchy and top-down direction, and far greater emphasis on bottom-up innovation and rapid market response. It means far greater emphasis to in-house education and training over the working life of employee-participants in enterprise activities.

In cultures based primarily upon individualism, and boosted by a midcentury obsession with the virtues of narcissism, it will be difficult to change economic habits, whether in the workplace or in the stratospheric levels of corporate and government leadership. But it seems doubtful whether competitiveness can be assured in any other way, and especially doubtful whether it can be achieved by counting upon greater government involvement in economic activities of enterprises, or in shielding them from external shocks and disturbances.

The future prospects of existing enterprises and industries in many nations seem gloomy in this perspective—especially in the centrally planned economies, and in those developing nations where governments dominate economic decision making. For the centrally planned economies, global economic change in the next few years will clearly outpace the old top-down decision processes that characterize these economies. The fundamental question is not whether there will be economic reform, as is already under way in the framework of *perestroika*, but rather whether reform will be fast enough. For the developing countries, the traditional foundations for economic growth, such as cheap labor and abundant natural resources, will generally not be a sufficient basis for growth and maintenance of competitiveness in the next decade. Governments that try to shape economic change to fit these traditional parameters will risk failure.

But the rapid emergence of new technologies already in the currents of history assures great potential for higher growth and enhanced well-being in the industrialized nations of the West, and especially in the United States, the European Community, and in Japan. Whether this potential is realized depends upon whether our societies can alter perspectives about our economic organizations and our choices between future benefits and present consumption. In essence, whether individuals, enterprises, or nations can realize this potential depends upon whether we can lift our eyes away from our feet and look into the future with greater confidence.

5

The Metamorphosis of the Third World: U.S. Interests in the 1990s

JOHN W. SEWELL

Introduction

As the United States enters the last decade of the twentieth century, it faces a policy environment unprecedented in postwar history. The U.S. economy is still the world's largest and wealthiest, but the heightened interdependence of the in-

JOHN W. SEWELL has been president of the Overseas Development Council since 1980. He joined the ODC staff in 1971 as vice president and served as executive vice president from 1977 to 1979. Prior to joining the ODC, Mr. Sewell worked at The Brookings Institution, and served in the U.S. Foreign Service and in the Research Bureau of the Department of State. Mr. Sewell has written several publications about Third World development and U.S. interests, and he often lectures at major universities, government agencies, and private institutions.

ternational system has eroded the ability of the United States unilaterally to dictate its own interests.

Unlike earlier periods, the developing countries are much more central to important U.S. interests. The developing world, however, also has changed, and U.S. relations with the developing countries in the 1990s will be played out in a much different policy environment than in the past.

The United States has interests in the developing world in the 1990s that are multiple, complex, overlapping, and often conflicting. Economic and political interests in many developing countries will sharpen, and security interests—as traditionally defined—may diminish.

The diminution of security interests is in and of itself a major change, as U.S. policies toward the developing countries have been dominated by concerns about military security since the 1950s. Hopefully, the evolving U.S.–Soviet relationship will reduce threats to American interests in the Third World and open diplomatic possibilities to reduce tensions. Several factors may lead the Soviets to reach at least de facto agreements on Third World issues with the Bush administration. First, military expenditures and subsidies to Third World client states drain needed resources out of the Soviet economy. The recent negotiations among South Africa, Cuba, and Angola (with U.S. mediation) over independence for Namibia are an example of a flashpoint's being defused with U.S. and Soviet cooperation. Second, the Soviets have become increasingly skeptical about the Third World's potential for revolution, and commentators have expressed doubts about the near-term potential for communism in the Third World. Third, the Soviets seem to be interested in the middle-income countries more as trading partners and competitors than as clients. Soviet Foreign Minister Eduard Shevardnadze's fall 1987 trip to Brazil, Argentina, and Uruguay to boost trade and diplomatic relations between the Soviet Union and Latin America is an indication of this emerging policy.

Soviet interest in participating in international agencies and organizations, such as the General Agreement on Tariffs and

Trade (GATT), the International Monetary Fund (IMF), the World Bank, and the United Nations, also may present an opportunity for enhancing relationships with the Soviet Union. Participating in these institutions would increase the Soviet stake in the international system, and could broaden the superpower relationship along multilateral lines.

This chapter is based on the assumption that traditional U.S. international economic interests that have been sustained in the postwar period are valid; and that U.S. interests lie in fostering an expanding and relatively open global trading and financial system that meets the needs of all countries that participate in it. In addition, the United States now has an urgent interest in ameliorating a set of common global problems— poverty, environment, population, acquired immune deficiency syndrome (AIDS), and drugs—that in different ways threaten our own well-being.

In the decade ahead, however, the United States no longer has the power to dominate and "manage" the international system by itself; and currently it is constrained by its own economic mismanagement. In addition, the developing countries must be more centrally involved if the United States is to further its own interests. In the last two decades many developing countries have:

- emerged as important trading partners—particularly as export markets at a time when trade has become more important to the United States—and as competitors in manufactured goods, such as steel, autos, and light aircraft.
- become important participants in the international financial system, most notably as borrowers from the commercial banking systems of the industrialized world.
- emerged as politically important in their own right. Few countries are as important to the United States as is its neighbor, Mexico.
- developed much greater capacities to manage their own affairs, and are less likely to be dictated to from abroad.

• become important potential partners in addressing the international "global agenda" problems of poverty and environment, and common social concerns, such as narcotics and AIDS.

The "Third World" Has Changed and the Pace of Change Will Continue

From 1950 to 1980 the developing countries compiled a spectacular record of economic growth. As a group, they grew at a faster rate in the postwar period than the developed countries did during their own industrial revolutions. As a result, the developing country share in real gross world product grew from 15 percent in 1960 to 22 percent in 1985. In the same period, many of these countries became important participants in the expanding global trading system. In 1965 they accounted for only 7 percent of exports of manufacturers; by 1985 their share of global manufactured exports had risen to over 16 percent.

The composition of Third World industrial exports also changed, with traditional labor-intensive products, such as shoes and textiles, diminishing in importance compared to exports of electric machinery, chemicals, and transport equipment. In 1986, for the first time, developing countries as a whole earned more foreign exchange selling manufactured exports than fuels or nonfuel primary products. Manufactures now account for more than one-half the foreign exchange earnings of large middle-income countries, such as the Philippines and Thailand.

But economic progress has been shared unevenly among developing countries, and there is now a growing differentiation among and between countries.

In the 1960s and 1970s Latin America experienced quite respectable growth, particularly in countries such as Brazil and Mexico. And a number of other middle-income countries succeeded in enhancing their status in the international economy.

But Asia is the real success story. Between 1970 and 1986 the newly industrialized Asian countries outpaced average world trade and output growth. Real output of these economies increased at an annual average of 6 to 8 percent between 1980 and 1987. The volume of merchandise exports of the newly industrialized Asian countries expanded at an average of about 12.7 percent a year between 1980 and 1987, or more than three times as fast as world merchandise trade volume. In 1986 (according to GATT calculations in *International Trade 1986–87*) the dollar value of Asian countries' merchandise exports increased by 13 percent to reach $465 billion, or about 22 percent of world merchandise exports. Asian countries' trade surpluses rose as the volume of their imports lagged far behind exports in the 1980s.

In contrast the low-income countries—concentrated in sub-Saharan Africa, but also in South Asia and Latin America—have remained producers of primary commodities and are heavily dependent on flows of concessionary resources. But even sub-Saharan Africa posted respectable records of economic growth in the 1960s and early 1970s.

In the 1970s the pattern of financial flows to the developing countries also changed; total transfers grew rapidly and diversified. Private bank lending (fueled by surpluses from the Organization of Petroleum Exporting Countries—OPEC) and foreign investment swamped Official Development Assistance (ODA). Resource flows from OECD (Organization for Economic Cooperation and Development) nations to developing countries nearly tripled between 1970 and 1983. In the five years prior to 1982, developing countries received positive net resource transfers of $147 billion in medium- and long-term lending—with most of the increase coming from private commercial sources. As a result, by 1983 Official Development Assistance accounted for less than one-third of total financial flows from rich to poor countries.

This progress came to a halt in most parts of the developing world in the early 1980s, and in terms of economic growth, the 1980s have been a lost decade. Only Asia has escaped.

High interest rates, falling commodity prices, heavy debt burdens, negative net transfers, volatile exchange rates, and restricted markets in the developed economies plagued a faltering international economy. World recession, and then crippling debt-service payments, caused growth among Latin American countries to slow to annual average rates of 1.9 percent between 1980 and 1987. Per capita income is roughly 8 percent lower today than in 1981, and wages have dropped by 30 to 40 percent in some countries. Sub-Saharan Africa grew more slowly than other developing regions in the 1970s, and the situation worsened drastically over the period from 1980 to 1987 as Africa's real gross domestic product grew by less than two-tenths of one percent annually. As national income dropped and populations climbed, per capita incomes in some African countries have fallen by as much as 25 percent since 1981. Like Latin America, Africa's export performance continues to be plagued by restrictive debt burdens and a lack of net capital inflows. Moreover, the sharp decline in prices of primary products, which comprise 90 percent of the region's exports, slashed export earnings.

According to most forecasts for the period to 1995, developing country growth will remain restrained. The World Bank projects real gross domestic product growth for developing countries as a group at about 4.2 percent—higher than earlier this decade, but significantly below the rate achieved during the 1970s. Low-income countries' growth rates—particularly for sub-Saharan Africa—are expected to be barely sufficient to keep pace with population increases. World Bank forecasts suggest that under less than optimistic conditions, per capita gross domestic product growth in Africa will be zero for the first half of the 1990s.

As a result of these changes, both favorable and unfavorable, the construct of the "developing world" is itself no longer adequate as a basis for defining U.S. interests and determining U.S. policies. Indeed, these countries now exhibit such diversity as to raise questions about the validity of the very concept. The developing world now can be disaggregated for purposes of policy analysis into at least three rough groupings; but even these contain a wide diversity of countries:

- the *industrializing countries,* including the six newly industrial-izing countries of East Asia and Latin America, but also a much larger number of countries that have increased their industrial production as a share of gross domestic product;
- the *low-income countries* of sub-Saharan Africa, South Asia, and Latin America;
- the *"Giants"*—India and China—that are rapidly moderniz-ing industrial economies held back by large rural and still very poor populations.

Each of these categories, however, encompasses a variety of countries. The "industrializing" category includes the Asian countries, which have piled up substantial financial reserves, and the debt-burdened economies of Brazil and Mexico in Latin America. Similarly, Kenya, Zimbabwe, and the Ivory Coast in Africa have compiled very respectable records of in-creasing manufactured output based on their agricultural re-sources. Finally, countries in all these categories face prob-lems of poverty and environmental deterioration.

In the 1990s policy makers should look at the developing countries not by income categories, but by the issue areas in which individual countries are important to U.S. interests. For instance, discussions on commercial debt should mainly in-volve Latin America, as only a few African countries borrowed from commercial banks; trade negotiations should touch on various groups of developing countries, depending on the par-ticular trade issue; and U.S. foreign aid should be concen-trated in the countries that do not have access to global mar-kets or nonconcessional capital.

The Changed Position
of the United States

The health of the U.S. economy will have immense implica-tions for the policy environment of the 1990s, and therefore for U.S. relations with the developing countries. As the United States still accounts for 28 percent of the world's gross national product (GNP), an expanding U.S. economy can create an international environment conducive to progress and growth; but a faltering U.S. economy cannot provide the markets necessary to absorb growing developing country exports, and will not have the resources needed to deal with the issue and assist renewed growth and progress in the developing countries.

The United States, however, now is in an international economic position unprecedented since 1945. Like many debt-burdened developing countries, the United States must balance its trade accounts, service its foreign debt, and rebuild its industrial base. Although its position is undeniably more favorable than that of any developing country, the United States, too, needs to develop.

Most analysts believe that the external deficit of the United States can be brought under control and the U.S. economic position restored only with a substantial reduction in the federal budget deficit. Equally important, coordinated policy action by the main industrial economies, particularly Japan and Germany, will be needed to reduce trade imbalances to sustainable levels, to avoid a recession in the United States, and to set the stage for steady growth worldwide during the next decade.

Conventional wisdom currently holds that the U.S. trade imbalance will be closed if these measures are taken. The role that could be played by the developing countries—or, more specifically, by the countries that are important participants in the international economy—is virtually absent from current policy discussions. According to Overseas Development Council (ODC) estimates, however, renewed growth in those countries could raise U.S. exports to developing countries by as much as $30 billion by 1992 (John W. Sewell, "The Dual Challenge: Managing the Economic Crisis and Technological Change," in *Growth, Exports, & Jobs in a Changing World Economy: Agenda 1988*). The industrialized countries of Western Europe present only modest opportunities for increased U.S. exports.

Even under optimistic assumptions about increased openness in Japan, that country is not large enough to be the only expanding market for U.S. exports.

ODC's analysis shows that resumed growth in the industrialized countries will be necessary but not by itself sufficient to increase U.S. exports and reduce the U.S. trade deficit to manageable proportions. In addition, the current debt-induced outflow of resources from the developing countries will have to be reversed to expand developing country import capacity—and our own export potential. Contrary to the thrust of the current debate raging in this country, U.S. trade problems with most developing countries are far more due to their current debt predicament and weakened import capability than to either unfair trade practices or any fundamental decline in U.S. competitiveness.

The hard fact is that neither the U.S. merchandise trade account nor the current account is likely to be balanced in the next several years. But sustained and rapid growth in the industrializing developing countries is a key element in making significant progress toward reducing the trade deficit without inducing a global recession.

The Emergence of a Global Agenda of Interrelated Problems

Along with growth, debt, and adjustment, poverty, environmental sustainability, rapid population growth, urbanization, AIDS, and drugs are now central issues in U.S. relations with the developing countries.

Poverty

Just as developing countries made important advances in economic growth during the 1960s, important achievements also were made in human well-being. Life expectancy rose and infant mortality rates fell in most developing countries. People in developing countries in 1985 could expect to live an aver-

age of about sixty years, compared to about fifty-one years in
1965. Literacy has spread dramatically: primary school education is now a reality for most children in the developing world,
and secondary school enrollment rates have also improved.

Nevertheless, the problem of poverty looms larger than
ever. Despite measurable progress, the stark reality is that the
poor are still very poor, and, because of population growth,
there are now more of them. Roughly one in five of this
planet's 5 billion people lives in absolute poverty, struggling
with malnutrition, illiteracy, disease, infant mortality, and
short life expectancy. In addition, a disproportionate number
of people living in poverty are women, posing a new challenge
for those concerned with alleviating poverty. In a September
1988 address to the World Bank Board of Governors, Barber
Conable, president of the World Bank, pointed out:

Poverty on today's scale prevents a billion people from having even a
minimally acceptable standard of living. To allow every fifth human
being on our planet to suffer such an existence is a moral outrage. It is
more: It is bad economics, a terrible waste of precious development
resources. Poverty destroys lives, human dignity and economic potential.

The incidence of poverty varies markedly from region to
region. In East and Southeast Asia, slower population growth
rates and steady advances in per capita income have contributed to a significant reduction in poverty. In South Asia, where
roughly half of the world's poor live, modest rates of growth
have barely kept pace with the expanding population. And in
sub-Saharan Africa, where two-thirds of the people live in poverty, rapid population growth rates combined with sustained
economic deterioration, falling or stagnant agricultural production, and natural disasters all have contributed to widespread malnutrition and decreased social welfare.

In addition, the economic stagnation of most developing
countries in the 1980s has reversed many hard-won gains of
earlier decades. For sixteen African and Latin American countries, per capita income was lower in 1985 than in 1965. In

another dozen countries in these two regions, per capita income grew by less than 1 percent during the same period. In twenty African countries, the average calorie supply, already inadequate, was lower in 1985 than in 1965. With slow growth predicted for most of these economies in the 1990s, the prospects for recovery of living standards in the future is questionable.

Environment

Massive and potentially irreversible environmental destruction is consuming the earth's resource base. Between 1950 and 1983, 38 percent of Central America's and 24 percent of Africa's forests disappeared. Logging, agricultural expansion, and urban growth contributed to the destruction of forests. Deforestation undermines development by destroying watersheds, reducing fuel and material availability, destroying species, and affecting global climate.

The temperature of the earth's atmosphere appears to be rising, posing a serious threat to virtually all natural processes on which human life depends. The so-called greenhouse effect expected to result from rising atmospheric concentrations of carbon dioxide and other gases is already under way. Between 1950 and 1983 the level of carbon dioxide emissions tripled. The largest portion is due to industrialized countries, but the fastest growth of emissions has been in developing countries.

The report of the World Commission on Environment and Development, chaired by Norwegian Prime Minister Gro Brundtland, concluded that

Major unintended changes are occurring in the atmosphere, in soils, in waters, among plants and animals, and in the relationships among all of these. The rate of change is outstripping the ability of scientific disciplines and our current capabilities to assess and advise: The security, well-being, and very survival of the planet depends on making the necessary institutional changes, now

Population

Environmental problems are exacerbated by population growth. Each of the 86 million people added to the population each year will consume additional land, water, and energy, thus further straining the environment. The world's population doubled in less than thirty years, passing the 5 billion mark in 1987. An additional 3 billion people will inhabit the globe by 2025.

Almost all of the growth in global populations has been concentrated in the developing world, where human demands often overtax local systems. Although population growth per se is not always harmful, when annual population increases are coupled with heightened stress on local ecosystems, shortages of food, fodder, and fuel can emerge almost overnight. If the demands of local populations surpass the sustainable yields of forests, grasslands, and croplands, the systems will continue to deteriorate even if population growth stops. Shortages of fuelwood—which affect 1.5 billion people in sixty-five countries—and the search for crop and pasture land contribute to the rampant devastation. In India, well over half the lands suffer from degradation and face steadily declining productivity without major new investments.

Urbanization

Since 1950 Third World cities have been growing approximately three times faster than those in the industrialized world. By the turn of the century, half of the world's population will be urban, and eighteen of the world's twenty-one largest cities will be located in the developing world. Third World cities are growing very fast, but squatter settlements, shantytowns, and low-income neighborhoods within cities are growing about twice as fast. In the poorest countries, such as Haiti and Burundi, as many as one-half of all city dwellers live in absolute poverty; in India, about 40 percent; and in less poor countries, such as Morocco or the Philippines, about 30 percent.

Common Social Problems: AIDS and Drugs

An increasing share of the global total of AIDS cases has been identified in developing countries where limited resources inhibit the ability to respond to the AIDS challenge with effective prevention campaigns. In per capita terms, a number of developing countries already have statistically more severe AIDS epidemics than does the United States. Globally, AIDS epidemics appear to be most serious in Africa, the Caribbean, Europe, and North America—with seventeen of the nineteen most afflicted countries found in Africa and the Caribbean. In Uganda, for example, the number of people with AIDS may be doubling every four to six months, and if present rates continue, more than half of all sexually active Ugandans may be infected by 2000.

The impact of AIDS on social and economic development in the developing world, though difficult to forecast, may be critical. A preliminary study by Harvard University showed that economic losses due to AIDS in five seriously affected central African countries could begin to exceed total foreign aid to those countries by 1991. Poor health resulting from poverty may intensify the impact of AIDS in many developing countries, since malnutrition increases a person's susceptibility to infectious disease.

The rising tide of illicit drugs entering developed country markets represents a significant and increasingly divisive factor in relations with the developing world. The main consumer countries are rich and industrialized; the main producer countries are poor and predominantly agricultural. Producer and consumer countries blame each other for the accelerating drug traffic and advocate, respectively, demand-side and supply-side solutions. Efforts to control drug cultivation and production overseas often impinge on nationalist sensitivities. Political elites in some developing countries view antidrug crusades as imposing significant economic and social costs and as creating new and formidable political challenges. Inevitably, narcotics control drains political and financial capital that could be used to pursue other policy goals.

A "Third Industrial Revolution" May Transform Relations Between Developed and Developing Countries

If the United States deals with its immediate economic problems and adjusts to a changed international economic position, it can end up in a relatively more powerful position by the mid-1990s.

This does not mean, however—as some seem to assume—that if the adjustment task is accomplished, the world will revert to the *status quo ante.* Nor is it clear that, even if the United States makes the transition, prospects for many developing countries will be particularly favorable. Not only do they have to work their way out of the debt situation; but at the same time, developments in economics, environment, science, technology, and industrial organization are rapidly changing the structure of the international economy, with profound implications for both the United States and the developing countries.

Technological developments, such as qualitative advances in information processing, industrial robots, and new high-speed global communications networks, are contributing to fundamental shifts in relations between the United States and the developing countries. This "Third Industrial Revolution" has the potential to enable the United States to reestablish economic supremacy, but it also threatens to increase the gap between industrialized and developing countries. The prospect of a developing world lagging further and further behind technologically—and unable to compete globally on any significant scale—is not in the political and economic interests of the United States or the developing countries.

By the mid-1990s, the impact of the new industrial technolo-

gies will be felt. The components include virtually simulta-
neous developments:

- Micro electronics is drastically reshaping patterns of industrial production and already has led to the introduction of totally new products. Welding and painting in the
auto industry, for instance, are almost exclusively done by
robots.
- Leaps in global communications link together the world
virtually instantaneously, allowing industry to be geographically dispersed.
- New management techniques pioneered by the Japanese are
transforming industrial production in the United States.
These include "just-in-time" inventory practices, an emphasis on quality production, and the development of new,
closer links between suppliers and producers.
- Finally, new advanced synthetic materials developed for
specific purposes and the new products resulting from our
vastly expanded understanding of genetics already are appearing in the marketplace.

These technologies can work to the advantage of the United
States. American workers are skilled and flexible; and the U.S.
labor force will grow slowly between now and the year 2000.
U.S. research and development capacity is strong, and the
United States has Third World neighbors that can provide
close, lower-cost manufacturing sites. One major stumbling
block is the fact that these developments require capital and
technological skill, which developing countries lack. Likewise,
many of these new technologies require fewer workers. Yet a
country like Mexico faces the difficult choice between invest-
ing in these technologies to remain globally competitive, and
the need to create a million new jobs a year to accommodate its
growing population.

Developing countries that do not have a significant industrial base and that do not already export to industrialized
countries will find their economic problems compounded.
This poses tremendous challenges for the United States. If
these countries are not equipped to assimilate new technolo-

gies, their deepening economic malaise will exert the same kind of drag on American exports in the 1990s as it has since the early 1980s.

Policies for the 1990s

Choices taken in the period immediately ahead will determine the broad shape of the policy environment in the developing countries by the mid-1990s. There are various possible outcomes. At one extreme, a series of difficult policy decisions can be taken to deal with the debt issue and with continued liberalization of the global trading system that will restore economic growth rates in the developing countries (and the industrialized world) to levels approaching those of the 1960s and 1970s. At the other, global growth rates could well continue at the low levels of the 1980s, leading to widely divergent country experiences. Continuing population growth combined with stagnant economies could lead to a developing world containing many countries marked by increasing tension and growing human misery.

The current U.S. economic predicament has focused political attention on the need to take policy action swiftly. To revitalize its economy and restore its ability to exercise international leadership, the United States would be wise to devise measures to support renewed global growth, including rapid growth in the developing countries. In the immediate future, financial measures will be of utmost importance to this effort.

Meanwhile, however, the longer-term economic trends driven by the technological revolution continue unabated. The kinds of policies needed to address these problems generally have longer lead times than the short-term financial measures that can stimulate growth, making it imperative to proceed on both fronts at the same time. The following policy recommendations focus on measures to deal with the present economic crisis; measures to anticipate the now emerging, longer-term technological transformation are laid out elsewhere. (See my previously cited work.)

Managing the Short-Term Financial Crisis

The United States has a very strong interest in pursuing a short-term global economic strategy that emphasizes renewed global growth, particularly in the developing countries. Furthermore, if this growth is to have the necessary, positive impact on global trade imbalances, it is vital to design policy actions to help channel it into expanded trade. From the perspective of the United States as well as developing countries, these actions must pay particular attention to growth in developing countries. These policies will have to be developed and implemented in cooperation with other industrialized countries and with the developing countries most concerned. In this setting, U.S. leadership remains pivotal. The policies described below can be implemented only if the United States, despite its current economic problems, takes an active role in designing and supporting them.

The central short-term issue for U.S. policy makers is to identify politically feasible new initiatives to help the developing countries resume and sustain economic growth. The imperatives of narrowing the U.S. budget deficit currently make any major expansion of resources for international programs politically difficult. And the commercial banks and private equity investors are highly unlikely to expand current lending levels or strengthen their investment positions until growth resumes in those countries. But new programs are possible if the need is important enough.

Renewed and sustained growth in the developing countries requires that these countries themselves adopt appropriate economic policies, and that the net transfer of resources to those countries be at a level that supports growth.

A globally coordinated, U.S.–led debt policy designed to reverse the net drain of resources from the debtor countries is essential to this end. Such a policy should allocate the costs of adjustment among banks, debtor countries, international institutions, and lending countries without destabilizing the international banking system. A central element of such a strategy would be the establishment of target figures, perhaps under the aegis of the World Bank and International Monetary Fund, for individual debtor countries to reduce resource drains in ways supportive of more equitable economic growth. The strategy would include measures both to promote economic efficiency and to protect particularly vulnerable groups of poor people within developing countries. Creditors—whether governments, international financial institutions, or commercial banks—would have discretion to decide either to extend new loans or to cut debt-service requirements (Richard E. Feinberg, "Third World Debt and Development," in *Transition '89: Blueprints for America,* published by the Democracy Project). A strategy containing these elements not only would spread the costs of adjustment more equitably but would also considerably improve the U.S. trade balance, enhance American leadership in international economic relations, and improve U.S. diplomatic relations with the developing countries.

Management of the debt crisis will be a central issue well into the 1990s. The key to resumed growth is a combination of tough policy choices by developing countries, an amelioration of the debt situation as discussed earlier, and a heretofore elusive degree of global macroeconomic coordination. Sustained economic growth in the developing countries will be necessary to expand world trade and long-term investment. Leaders of the developed countries will need to take coordinated action to avoid volatility in exchange rates and in interest rates, and to ensure that their macroeconomic policy choices provide an environment for global growth.

If this growth strategy is to happen, policy makers will need to design creative ways to stimulate the flow of additional public and private resources to the developing countries. Among the steps that need to be taken are the following.

Increase Transfers from Countries in Surplus. Countries with large financial surpluses, most notably Japan, must begin to play a more important role in global finance. The Japanese government has expanded its aid program dramatically in recent years. Measured as a percentage of GNP, Japan's level of aid is already higher than that of the United States, and Japan has now passed the United States as the world's largest donor in absolute terms. But Japan has been reluctant to assume international economic leadership and generally has deferred to the United States. One of the creative challenges facing policy makers is to devise measures to encourage the Japanese and surplus countries in Western Europe to use more of their surpluses for restarting growth in the developing world. For both Japan and the United States, this task is not, however, without political problems. The Japanese surplus is largely in private hands, and measures will have to be devised to channel it to international purposes. The United States faces a different problem. The international financial institutions should have a major role to play in recycling these surpluses, but the United States would inevitably have to yield more of its influence in these institutions to the Japanese and other new contributors.

Generate New Resources with Minimal Budgetary Impact. The exigencies of the current crisis should stimulate policy makers to look for nontraditional ways of providing capital to restore growth in the major debtor countries. The current crisis also calls for more imaginative use of guarantees to foster greater capital flows and debt service reduction—as suggested by U.S. Treasury Secretary Nicholas Brady—into the developing countries. A special issuance of the Fund's Special Drawing Rights (SDRs) for allocation to developing countries under the aegis of the World Bank and the International Monetary Fund is another potential source.

Redirect Resources Available through the U.S. International Affairs Budget. The United States can restructure its existing international affairs budget to respond to these challenges. During the first half of this decade, this budget (generally known as the "foreign aid" program) more than doubled, but all of the increase has gone to military and security aid—to the neglect of programs designed to foster American interests in the developing countries through economic growth and long-term development. Economic and development assistance has in fact declined. The imbalance between the military and the economic in current programs represents a misallocation of scarce resources that the United States can no longer afford in this period of budgetary stringency. U.S. interests in the developing world today by and large do not stem from concerns about military security; they are largely economic, political, and humanitarian. Even a modest reallocation of funds within the current budget—in the range of 10 to 20 percent—could free a substantial amount of resources to support global growth in the developing countries.

Expand Trade. Policy makers will need to give priority to expanding exports to the developing countries, particularly to those that are rapidly industrializing. Trade will remain a priority whether or not the current round of trade negotiations is successfully completed in the early 1990s. Two quite different sets of policies will be important to that end. Some developing countries will continue to run surpluses and will need persuasion to open their markets to imports from both industrialized and developing countries; others, however, will still be working their way out from under the debt overhang through receiving trade surpluses. Their ability to import will depend on the availability of capital inflows.

Expand Exports. Ensuring the continued growth of export markets in the developing countries will have to remain a central priority of U.S. foreign policy throughout the 1990s. In industries such as microelectronics-based manufacturing and in agriculture, American producers need to look to markets in the developing countries for future growth. In the case of micro electronics, Manuel Castells and Laura D'Andrea Tyson argue (in "High-Technology Choices Ahead: Restructuring Interdependence," in *Growth, Exports, & Jobs in a Changing World Economy: Agenda 1988*):

In the long run, the incorporation of the Third World into global technology markets, both as users and as producers of microelectronics innovations, will increase market demand and the range of applications for such innovations. For many years to come, the major markets will remain in the North. Only if new policies are designed now, however, will we be able to see a gradual expansion of demand in the Third World.

In the case of agricultural exports, the world is not "awash in grain" due to increased agricultural production in the developing countries, but rather because developing countries lack import capacity. Indeed, the experience of the 1970s indicates that the potential is great for mutually beneficial market expansion for U.S. exports through more rapid development in the developing countries.

Other trade issues will loom large as a result of the changes in industrial technology and organization. These include the need to develop new rules to govern the disputes that will inevitably arise as more developing countries seek to take advantage of an open trade system, especially in the areas of intellectual property and investment promotion measures, and also as much more creative effort to increase trade among developing countries themselves.

Policies Toward Those Left Out: Poor People and Poor Countries

Despite the shifts that have gone on in relations between the United States and the developing countries, development assistance still will have a major role to play in the period ahead in promoting the development of the poorer nations and in addressing the global agenda issues described earlier. This will require considerable redesign and restructuring of current U.S. development cooperation policies.

Currently, only 40 percent of all aid from the OECD countries goes to the poor, low-income countries; the U.S. share going to lower-income countries is 24 percent. In most industrialized countries, budgetary resources for development assistance will be scarce, and the acute needs of the low-income countries make it imperative that concessional assistance be directed to them. The need for this shift is analogous to the importance of preserving a domestic "safety net" for disadvantaged groups in our own society, even in the face of economic adversity.

In addition, a new U.S. development cooperation program is needed that focuses on the address of a limited number of specific global problems, seeking to provide U.S. leadership in a concerted international effort by developed and developing countries to attack poverty and sustain the environment. It would be helpful to focus U.S. programs on internationally correlated and agreed upon goals for achievement by the end of the century to give focus to the programs and to attract public support. Possibilities include: food security and the significant reduction of chronic hunger; primary health care for a majority of the world's people on a sustainable basis; literacy for the new generations of children without discrimination on the basis of sex; halving existing high population growth rates; helping to build capacity in the developing countries to adapt and to utilize for their own revolutionary scientific and technological developments; and institutional development, education, and training to improve the capacity of developing countries to better manage their own environment and natural resources.

A concrete problem-solving mode of operation is important because U.S. resources are limited and represent a declining proportion of larger aid flows from other donors, and because developing countries themselves have acquired the competency to implement their own development choices.

U.S. leadership and leveraging on selected global problems would be a key element in a new development cooperation strategy, both in bilateral and multilateral aid programs, as well as on broader international economic policies. A much stronger leadership on donor coordination will provide the United States with greater influence on the amount and direction of resources provided, as well as on the content of programs of other donors and the multilateral development institutions.

In the 1990s, aid policies also will need to be radically redesigned to take account of the technological revolution and to ensure that its benefits do not bypass low-income countries and poor people. Countries that do not already have an industrial base and do not already export to the industrialized countries will find it increasingly difficult to compete in world markets unless they have some particular resource—material, human, or geographic—that will give them an edge. Low-income countries by and large will not be able to reap the benefits of the new industrial technology. In addition, past experience with dramatic technological innovations—most notably, some of the lessons learned in the introduction of the successful "Green Revolution" crops—illustrates that such innovations must be very carefully launched so as to avoid increasing social inequity.

The precise impact of the new technologies is still very difficult to predict; they are not yet in widespread use in developing countries, and their potential for improving human well-being through applications to health, education, and agriculture is far from fully understood. There is, moreover, a strong possibility that at least some of their side-effects will be adverse, especially in the near term. The reason lies in the nature of the technology. Fewer new jobs will be created, and those that are will be at a higher skill level—for which the majority of people in the developing world will not be qualified. As a result, in countries that achieve competitiveness, middle-class workers benefiting from the new technologies are likely to form "islands of prosperity," with a resulting aggravation of income disparities within the country.

On the other hand, the potential of the new technologies for vastly improving human well-being is also great. The microelectronics technology can be applied to development problems in even the poorest countries. For instance, remote sensing by satellites can be used for identifying resources, demographic planning, and early warning of drought. Personal computers can have a great impact on government planning and data collection, as is already the case in Nigeria and Kenya. The new telecommunications technologies make remote areas more accessible, permitting village-level education to spread widely and inexpensively. The new developments in biotechnology have vast potential for improving human welfare. As mentioned earlier, these include a range of new agricultural products, vaccines and medicines, and new sources of energy. Many potential biotechnology applications are of great significance for developing countries because they are relatively less capital-intensive, less energy-demanding, and less sophisticated than most of the current physical-chemical industrial methods.

Lessons for Policy Makers

The United States is entering a new era. Policy makers cannot ignore the constraints that the changed international economic position of the United States imposes on a broad range of its foreign policy choices without causing further long-term erosion of this country's international position—or without condemning future generations of Americans to paying off an unprecedented level of foreign debt.

The changes in the policy environment have implications for policy makers as they begin the redesign of U.S. development cooperation programs and lay out broader international economic policies.

Most importantly, the United States will have to implement expansionary, noninflationary monetary policy in conjunction with budget cutting to avoid the recessionary impact of lowering the federal budget deficit. This requires coordination with the central banks of the major industrialized countries. In addition, leaders of the developed world will need to take coordinated action to avoid volatility of exchange rates and in interest rates, and to ensure that their macroeconomic policies provide an environment conducive to global growth. If the world drops into another major recession, the impact on the developing countries will be disastrous, with heavy costs to U.S. interests.

Addressing the debt crisis should have priority in U.S. relations with the developing world. Third World debt has altered international trade flows and added to the U.S. trade deficit by forcing developing nations to trim their imports. Debt has also become a central issue in America's relations with its hemispheric neighbors and with sub-Saharan Africa. The overall aim of U.S. policies toward the developing countries should be to stimulate the flow of resources needed to resume growth in those countries.

Sustained and rapid economic growth in the Third World, particularly in the middle-income developing countries, is now of direct importance to the United States because it could be a key element in making significant progress toward reducing the U.S. trade deficit without inducing a global recession. As a result of debt and slow growth in the developing world, U.S. exports to all developing countries dropped from $88 billion in 1980 to $78 billion in 1987. The impact on employment also was dramatic. The actual and potential employment loss (if exports had grown in the 1980s as they did in the 1970s) amounted to nearly 1.8 million U.S. jobs—or nearly 26 percent of total official unemployment in 1989.

Trade openness remains crucial both for the United States and the developing countries. The industrialized countries must fight protectionist impulses and bolster world export earnings and buying power. It will not be possible for the developing countries to grow and service their debts if they are denied access to markets for their goods. In turn, the U.S. trade deficit will not decrease substantially without increasing the purchasing power of the developing world.

The trend in the developing world toward democracy and market oriented policies needs to be supported. Democratic regimes typically attempt to reconcile the developmental goals of economic growth, decreasing income inequality, and management of external dependencies. But democracy has proven an elusive goal over the long run in most of the Third World. For that reason, it is important that democratization and "openness" in the developing world be assisted.

The new developments in science and technology present opportunities for U.S. development programs. The pace of change and the specific outcomes to arrive in the wake of technological developments are still unclear. Aid policies will need to be redesigned to take account of the technological revolution and to ensure that its benefits do not bypass poor people and poor countries. Aid programs need to focus on assisting developing countries, particularly the poorer ones, to strengthen their national capacity to develop and utilize new technologies for their own benefit.

The growth in the number of aid donors and the relative decline in U.S. development assistance actually opens opportunities for the United States but also implies that development policy must be much more strategic. Countries with large financial surpluses, most notably Japan, must play a more important role in global finance. The Japanese and surplus countries in Western Europe should be encouraged to recycle their surpluses for restarting growth in the developing world. This task is not without political problems. The international financial institutions (IFIs) should play a major role in recycling these surpluses; the United States would, however, inevitably have to yield more of its influence in these institutions to the Japanese and other new contributors.

In an era of scarce U.S. resources, greater U.S. participation in the IFIs also has the advantage of leveraging large amounts of lending with small amounts of cash.

In the next decade, U.S. bilateral aid programs will not be essential to middle-income countries' growth, but they will continue to play a major role in the development of the low-income countries. U.S. aid should be targeted predominantly on those countries.

The emerging "global agenda" of interrelated problems and their worldwide repercussions should set the agenda for the U.S. aid program in the 1990s. The importance of these global problems demands a vigorous national and international response. The United States is the logical candidate to spearhead the effort to deal effectively with this nascent global agenda through renewed leadership in the international organizations. This is one area in which U.S. actions and leadership will be more important than U.S. funds.

6

Regional Trading Blocs: Pragmatic or Problematic Policy?

C. MICHAEL AHO
AND
SYLVIA OSTRY

Introduction

Regional trading blocs are again in the news and are being advocated as pragmatic policy by some policy makers in

C. MICHAEL AHO is director of economic studies and director of the international trade project at the Council on Foreign Relations. He served as economic advisor to Senator Bill Bradley and was director of the Office of Foreign Economic Research at the U.S. Department of Labor. Mr. Aho has written or coauthored numerous publications on international trade and on the international economy.

SYLVIA OSTRY, senior research fellow at the University of Toronto and the Volvo Distinguished Visiting Fellow at the Council on Foreign Relations, was in 1985 appointed Canada's ambassador for multilateral trade negotiations and the prime minister's personal representative for the economic summit. She has served in several positions in the Canadian government and has authored and coauthored over seventy publications covering a range of empirical and policy-analytic subjects.

a world characterized by a stubborn stalemate over trade liberalization. Is there today an established trend toward regional or bilateral trading blocs? Clearly, a simple yes or no answer to this highly significant question is not in the cards. But in order to assess the implications of recent developments—especially the launch of Europe 1992 and the U.S.–Canada Free Trade Agreement—it is useful to sketch out some of the major changes in the international economic environment that are shaping the evolution of the world trading system, either by accident or by design.

Of these changes, the most significant for the present discussion has been the steady erosion of the General Agreement on Tariffs and Trade (GATT), the postwar guardian of liberalizing multilateral trade. A weakened and inadequate GATT has both spawned the pursuit of alternatives to multilateralism and been further weakened by that pursuit.

The erosion of the GATT since the early 1970s has taken the form of the so-called new protectionism, i.e., selective domestic or border nontariff measures (such as quantitative restrictions, voluntary export restraints, voluntary import expansion, domestic trade-distorting subsidies, etc.). In the 1970s the wellspring of protectionist pressures in the developed countries of the Organization for Economic Cooperation and Development (OECD) was the strong pressure for adjustment arising from the severe commodity and oil shocks: the rise of new players, especially in the Pacific; accelerating change in information technology; and the breakdown of the Bretton Woods system of fixed exchange rates. The process of structural adaptation was impeded by a number of government actions imposed mainly during the 1960s, which had the unintended effect of impairing the capacity to adjust, especially in Europe. Slower growth in the 1970s and the deep recession of the early 1980s also inhibited mobility and adaptation. The new protectionism was designed to slow or even halt the necessary adaptation to ongoing structural change.

In the 1980s the erosion of the GATT has continued. The

exchange rate misalignment and large global imbalances of the first half of the decade fanned protectionist fires in the United States and fostered an increasing use of so-called process protectionism, i.e., quasi-judicial mechanisms to discourage imports or promote exports. Later in the decade, as pressures from exchange rate misalignment abated and the OECD countries undertook significant *domestic* policy action to liberalize markets by deregulation, privatization, etc., which significantly improved growth potential and reduced inflation, the scope of managed trade expanded in both industry and country coverage and was increasingly directed against each other and the newly industrializing economies (NIEs).

Now one is beginning to discern a possible innovation in the new protectionism (the new new protectionism?) in a shift from defensive import protection of mature industries to a combined domestic and border policy package aimed at protecting and fostering "strategic" industries undergoing rapid technological change. Perhaps the best indication of this new "infant prodigy" rationale is the innovative approach to antidumping regulation of the European Community (EC), which has been utilized recently, especially with respect to imports from Japan and the NIEs. A harbinger of the future in the United States, also involving antidumping in a strategic sector, could well be the U.S.–Japanese semiconductor dispute that resulted in a cartel-like arrangement.

The erosion of the GATT by the persistent but largely invisible shift to managed trade was exacerbated by the failure of U.S. efforts to launch a new GATT round early in the decade. It took four years after the near-collapse of the U.S.–promoted November 1982 GATT ministerial meeting (which foundered over the issues of agriculture and services) to reach agreement to launch the Uruguay Round. The ostensible reason for the delay was the opposition of a small group of developing countries led by Brazil and India, which opposed the inclusion of the so-called new issues of trade and investment—all key issues of increasing importance where GATT coverage was minimal or nonexistent. But this opposition probably could not

have prevented the launch had the three major trading partners (the pillars)—the United States, Japan, and the European
Community—been able to agree on timing; the disagreement
between the United States and the EC stemmed largely from
the political and institutional complexity of the trade policy
formulation process of the Community. The process is inevitably cautious and lengthy but was acutely contentious at this
time because a central issue of the negotiating agenda (unlike
previous GATT rounds) was agriculture, a subject of deep
divisiveness among member states, although one that is often
proclaimed to be the cement that keeps the Community together.

Efforts were made to move the process forward but to no
avail. The need for a greater international discipline and for a
prompt launch for new multilateral talks was cogently presented in the GATT Wisemen's Report, *Trade Policies For a
Better Future,* which argued, "Today the world market is not
opening up; it is being choked by a growing accumulation of
restrictive measures. Demands for protection are heard in
every country, and from one industry after another." The report also called for a strengthened GATT with new surveillance powers and institutional reforms. But it was precisely the
weakness of GATT as an institution without a forum to review
the recommendations that nullified any impact so that the
stalemate over the launch continued.

It is not possible, obviously, to say whether an earlier launch
of the Uruguay Round would have served to stem and perhaps
even partly reverse the steady march to managed trade in the
1980s. A multilateral trade negotiation has been a traditional
remedy, by and large successful, for diverting or deferring
protectionist claims in all countries, so the presumption is that
it would have been helpful in that regard. It is not accidental that although Section 301 has been on the books since the
U.S. Trade Act of 1974, it was only from 1985 that the statute was used aggressively to open foreign markets in specific
sectors.

But more to the point, perhaps, is that the world did not

stand still and wait for the Uruguay Round to begin. Major developments such as the U.S.–Canada Free Trade Agreement and the launch of the European Community Single Market (Europe 1992, as it is now popularly termed) got under way. But these were not the only developments that took place outside the GATT. The increasing importance of strengthening intellectual property rights in a period of accelerating technological change, not only in information technology but also in biogenetics and new materials, created strong pressures by business in the industrialized world for government action. Since the GATT was nonoperational for all intents and purposes in this vital area, bilateral action was the only option. To some extent the same circumstances governed policy in services, especially financial services, where bilateral agreements have proliferated. The culmination of U.S. trade policy pressures in the Omnibus Act of 1988 signaled that protectionism is not dead but quiescent: there is plenty of scope for process protectionism if the Bush administration is so inclined, and alternatives to multilateralism are well provided for should the Uruguay Round deliver less, less quickly than required.

Thus the erosion and inadequacy of the GATT and the delay in the launch of the Uruguay Round either unleashed or failed to stem a number of fundamental changes that further eroded the credibility and authority of multilateralism as the "consensus paradigm" governing world trade. Weakness begat weakness. In recognition of this situation, the agenda of the Uruguay Round is the most comprehensive and ambitious since the founding of the GATT, covering the unsolved problems of yesterday (especially agriculture, but also safeguards in textiles and clothing); the new issues of today and tomorrow (services, intellectual property, and investment); the reform of GATT as a contract (dispute settlement); and the first effort since Havana to add an institutional face to the "interim agreement" (the functioning of the GATT system, or FOGS).

One might be tempted to remark that all this could well be too much, too late. But the eventual answer to the question "is there today a trend toward bilateral or regional trading blocs?" will depend on the outcome of the Uruguay Round, for what is really on the table is multilateralism. The experience of the delayed launch and the Montreal midterm in December 1988, which put the Round "on hold" because the EC and the United States could not resolve their fundamental conflict over trade in agriculture, points up sharply the extraordinary difficulty of systemic reform in a world lacking an undisputed hegemon.

Some Definitions

Before proceeding to a full statement of the current context and the options available, it is useful to begin with definitions of critical terms: reciprocity, most favored nation treatment (MFN), free trade areas, trade creation, and trade diversion.

Reciprocity is an ambiguous term in international relations. According to Arthur Dunkel, the director-general of GATT:

> Reciprocity is always a subjective notion which cannot be looked at in bilateral terms. It cannot be determined exactly. It can only be agreed upon and such an agreement is possible only among countries sharing a commitment to some higher principle . . . the rule of law. . . . One side alone cannot decide what reciprocity is.

The principle Dunkel was referring to is nondiscrimination or most favored nation treatment combined with national treatment as it pertains to trade.

Economist Robert Keohane distinguishes between specific and diffuse reciprocity. Specific reciprocity refers to exchanges of items of equivalent value between specified partners. Obligations are clearly specified in terms of each country's rights and duties. Diffuse reciprocity refers to situations in which equivalence is less strictly defined, and partners in exchanges may be viewed as a group rather than individually.

According to Keohane, diffuse reciprocity is exemplifed by unconditional most favored nation treatment where norms and obligations are important. Specific reciprocity is exemplified by conditional MFN where country A extends to country B the same concessions it granted to country C *only if* country B reciprocates with concessions "equivalent" to those given by C to A. Conditional MFN can be used to expand trade and enhance discipline, but because only a limited number of countries are included, it is not the best that could be attained (although it may be much better than doing nothing). Specific reciprocity can also be narrow, not applied on a conditional MFN basis, and more aggressive as when countries negotiate tit-for-tat on a bilateral basis. Aggressive reciprocity is less likely to expand trade and enhance discipline and may, in fact, undermine discipline since it tends to be used in a discriminatory manner. The recent use of Section 301 of the Trade Act of 1974 by the United States and the proposed use of reciprocity by the European Community in its implementing directives to compete in the internal market are but two examples of narrow reciprocity that are less likely to be trade-creating on balance.

Although MFN is the centerpiece of the GATT system, that system also includes agreements involving conditional treatment. Some of the Tokyo Round nontariff barrier codes contain conditional MFN features. Only firms from countries that are signatories of the government procurement code may bid on the government projects that are open to foreign bids. Under U.S. law, only GATT members that are signatories of the subsidies code are entitled to the injury test on subsidized exports to the United States. These departures from MFN were designed to enhance discipline and therefore to be trade-promoting. They were also established to minimize free riding and to put pressure on foot draggers that were seeking to lower standards.

Other departures from unconditional MFN do not necessarily promote trade or enhance discipline. Regional groupings such as free trade areas and customs unions divert trade as well as create it (e.g., imports come from a higher-cost source of supply). GATT Article XXIV, which permits regional groupings, has been much abused. It lays out specific requirements that are seldom met in practice, although the 1988 U.S.–Canadian agreement is an exception. A further proliferation of regional groupings could set precedents for further special deals, fragment the trading system, and damage the interests of nonparticipants.

Before discussing the drawbacks of a bilateral or regional approach, it is worthwhile to review arguments in favor of an unconditional MFN approach. These arguments fall broadly into two categories, economic and political, with some overlap between the two. The economic arguments center on efficiency. Nondiscrimination among sources of supply minimizes the distortions from market efficiency because imports can come from the lowest-cost source. MFN also leads to more overall trade liberalization because liberalizing measures are generalized to cover all countries that are parties to the agreement. And, MFN is simple to administer so that transaction costs at the border are reduced.

The political arguments for unconditional MFN center around how it tends to reduce tension among nations. From an international political viewpoint, MFN fosters sovereign equality among nations and guarantees newcomers access to international markets. The automatic extension of trade-liberalizing measures to others reduces friction and disputes. In contrast, discriminatory arrangements can increase misunderstandings and disputes among different trade groupings or cause resentment on the part of outsiders. Discriminatory treatment also increases the probability that trade will be used as a weapon of foreign policy.

From a domestic political viewpoint, discriminatory restrictions are more difficult to remove because they create vested interests in exporting as well as importing countries. For example, both protected domestic textile producers and supplying firms in other countries that hold quota licenses find discriminatory restrictions to their benefit. Finally, MFN simplifies the legal and legislative burdens that proliferate if different countries are treated unequally. Discrimination often results in domestic laws being applied differently to imports from various origins. Separate national agreements increase the work of elected officials in countries, like the United States, where agreements have to be ratified by legislators. Legislative action on separate agreements also opens up the possibility of domestic political bargaining and logrolling, which could undermine the original intentions of the agreement.

The Triggers

The two major developments of regional trading arrangements that, in fact, seem to have triggered the current discussion about blocs are the 1988 U.S.–Canada Free Trade Agreement (FTA) and the EC move to dismantle impediments to the free flow of goods, services, capital, and labor among member states by the end of 1992.

The FTA and Europe 1992 are very different in both genesis and nature. Indeed, their coincidence in timing is accidental, not planned. Yet both are highly significant developments in the world trading system, which will foster increasing economic integration in the two largest and richest markets of the world. So it is probably not surprising that, despite their marked differences, these two regional developments have provoked questions about a possible new trend in the world trading system. The outcome of policies is often very different from the plans of policy makers.

The origins of the FTA were quite dissimilar in the United States and Canada. In the United States, the bilateral initiative was spawned by a need to quell the rising tide of protectionist pressure and the frustration of the administration with the difficulties of launching a new round of multilateral negotiations. It was developed as a "strategic threat" policy to unblock the launch of the Round and to underline the significance of the "new issues"—services, investment, and intellectual property. It was intended to warn the foot draggers (especially the EC) and the opponents (the hard-line developing countries, especially Brazil and India) that there were feasible and attractive alternatives to the GATT.

Strategic threat policy is now a feature of U.S. policy stance. Thus U.S. Trade Representative Carla Hills, in her confirmation hearings, noted that while "retaliation cannot be the goal of our policy, the credible threat of retaliation provides essential leverage in our market-opening efforts." The reference is to the Omnibus Trade Act of 1988, and especially to Section 301 and the new "super" 301. The latter's ancestor is the ill-fated (but unmourned) Gephardt amendment, which would have required mandatory retaliation against trading partners with "excessive and unwarranted" trade surpluses. The present provision is clearly a much more benign version, but it is significant because it could well foster a propensity to bilateralism as a means of access to individual country markets.

For Canada, the proximate reason for the bilateral initiative was fear of mounting U.S. protectionism. But equally important for the much smaller Canadian economy were the long-term competitiveness benefits that would be spurred by structural change from trade liberalization and secure access to a dynamic market ten times its size. Further, if a GATT round should be launched, the FTA would provide valuable bargaining coinage as the relatively more protected Canadian markets would attract third countries seeking to erode U.S. preferences.

There have been a number of economic estimates of the FTA impact in Canada, which show significant increases in long-term national income coming from lower consumer and producer prices as well as improved productivity. In the case of the United States, the gains are much more limited because of the larger size of the U.S. market and the relatively lower level of tariff barriers.

The creation of the Single Market—Europe 1992—is, of course, an entirely different phenomenon. The EC is at present a customs union, with a common external tariff, unlike the FTA where there is no plan of convergence of Canadian and U.S. commercial policy. But Europe 1992 goes far beyond a customs union toward full integration involving not only trade in goods and services but free movement of capital and labor and significant convergence in macroeconomic policy.

While there were numerous factors, both political and eco-

nomic, at play in launching the move to full integration, the
external trading environment does not appear to have been a
major consideration—in sharp contrast, of course, to the genesis of the FTA. Moreover, this curious absence of external
considerations (the dog that didn't bark?) has by and large
persisted. It is no exaggeration to say that almost every measure specified in the 1985 European Commission White Paper
has, either directly or indirectly, implications for both the external trade and pattern of foreign direct investment in the
European Community, which were not spelled out or even
alluded to. Similarly, there was scarcely any relevant analysis
of the external impact contained in the gigantic Ceccini Report
so that estimates of the trade diversion and trade creation effects might be assessed.

A statement issued by the Commission in the fall of 1988
entitled "Europe 1992: Europe World Partner" was reassur-
ing in tone but short on detail. The result of this less-than-
transparent approach has been to create uncertainty and continuing debate within and outside the EC about the precise
nature of the external policy of Europe 1992. The lack of information on intentions and effects has given rise to fear and
suspicion in some quarters both by governments and private
business. In the latter case, some firms may well have assumed
that the safest route to trade with Europe is through investment, and such strategic decisions will not await 1992, so the
future pattern of trade and investment will be affected regard-
less of the precise policies that will eventually be spelled out by
the Commission.

There are two issues in external policy that have yet to be
resolved: the removal of present disparities in the import
regimes of member countries and their replacement by a unified set of import rules toward third countries; and the new
policy issues covered in the Uruguay Round, of which trade in
services is clearly of major importance. With respect to the
latter, the use of the term "reciprocity," never precisely defined, has been especially disturbing to many of those outside
Europe.

The uncertainty created by the lack of information is compounded by another factor of historical origin. The record of EC trade policy over a period of years from the creation of the original Community of the Six might be termed "eclectic" or, perhaps, a curate's egg (parts of it are excellent). In addition to the Common Agricultural Policy (highly trade protectionist and trade distorting), liberalization both internally and externally in successive GATT rounds has been accompanied by an increasing use of preferential or discriminatory policies, both regional and sectoral. The World Bank Development Report of 1987 lists eleven separate categories of developing countries with which the EC has different preferential arrangements. To this should be added, of course, the preferential arrangement with EFTA, the European Free Trade Association, and a continuing concern with the bilateral balances (reciprocity of *results*) vis-à-vis Japan. There almost seems to be, indeed, a preference for selectivity and managed trade that runs counter to the—largely American inspired—postwar blueprint for liberalized trade embodied in the GATT principle of MFN. This historical record has likely exacerbated the suspicion engendered by the policy of minimal information so far characterizing the movement to Europe 1992.

These regional developments in Europe and North America—unrelated but coincidental in time—have sparked the present debate on regional blocs. Further, in the Pacific area, not only have exports and imports surged in recent years, but major structural changes, spurred by the global adjustment process and especially by the appreciation of the yen, are accelerating regional integration via enhanced trade and investment linkages.

Japanese direct investment flows into the four Asian NIEs and the Association of Southeast Asian Nations (ASEAN) have tripled since the first half of the 1980s, and rising wage costs and currency appreciation have induced restructuring from the NIEs to ASEAN. Japan's market has become as important as that of the United States for the Asian NIEs as a pattern of horizontal specialization. Not surprisingly, in the light of this rapid economic evolution but also partly in response to European and North American developments, there is increasing interest in exploring regional trading arrangements among the non-Communist nations in the area, and a number of alternative options are being studied by both governments and private groups. Clearly, the political difficulties of institutional integration in the Pacific (even among the non-Communist countries) are immeasurably greater than in Europe—so much so that many observers discount the possibility of a free trade area, let alone a closer union. But the number of proposals emanating from the United States and elsewhere is in itself significant, and, as will be suggested below, the active pursuit of bilateralism and regionalism imposes a cost (in forgone resources and, more importantly, political commitment) on the alternative policy of reinforcing and updating the multilateral system.

Why are important policy makers in the United States advocating bilateral trade agreements, and, in particular, one with Japan? The proposals come on the heels of the Reagan administration's negotiation of a bilateral agreement with Canada, the largest trading partner of the United States. (A less comprehensive agreement was negotiated with Israel in 1985.) The Reagan administration deserves credit for successfully negotiating the pact with Canada, because it did signal that trade liberalization is still possible and that international negotiations can still bear fruit. The Canadian pact has gone further, faster than the multilateral GATT talks and was intended to be a catalyst for those talks.

But the impetus for bilateral trade agreements on the part of the United States grows out of substantial congressional frustration with the Reagan administration's trade policy and with its lack of progress in solving trade problems. Despite its basic ideological commitment to free trade, U.S. trade policy changed in some significant degree under the Reagan administration. George Bush will have to make trade a priority if he wants to resist protectionism at home and to minimize trade friction and open markets abroad.

As has been pointed out earlier, unprecedented trade deficits and unprecedented private sector complaints spawned unprecedented administrative and legislative action on trade in the years after 1985. In September 1985, after four years in which it repeatedly labeled the trade deficit a sign of economic strength, the Reagan administration changed course and began vigorous, if not always effective, action against allegedly unfair practices by foreign firms and foreign countries. It initiated over a dozen unfairness complaints (under Section 301 of the Trade Act of 1974) against countries accused of maintaining barriers to U.S. exports; negotiated a cartel-like semiconductor agreement with Japan; and then applied sanctions against Japan for allegedly violating the agreement.

According to then Treasury Secretary James A. Baker III, the Reagan administration provided more import relief than any of its predecessors in the past fifty years. Meanwhile, the U.S. Congress passed, over initial objections from the Reagan administration, a 1000-page trade reform bill, unprecedented in scope and scale.

So, while the Reagan administration took the leadership role in the Uruguay Round launch and agenda, at the same time a combination of forces (the global imbalances spawned by U.S. macroeconomic policy, the weakness of the GATT, the reluctance or opposition of major trading partners, and ongoing structural change in the global economy) set U.S. trade policy on what could be a new course.

George Bush will be under pressure to pursue a more active trade policy, mixing multilateral, bilateral, and unilateral initiatives. Some are urging the United States to unilaterally adopt a tit-for-tat trade policy, retaliating against alleged unfair trade practices or against countries with persistent surpluses, and, as noted, early signs from the Bush administration echo this view in part. How the 1988 Omnibus Trade Act will be implemented remains to be seen. One of the open questions is how its reciprocity provisions will be interpreted. Eventually the pressure will diminish as the depreciation of the dollar and the declining U.S. budget deficit (we hope) both work to reduce the trade deficit. (Then the protectionist pressures will shift to other regions of the world, especially to Europe and Japan.) But in the meantime, sentiment is growing for the United States to abandon its traditional multilateral approach to trade and to forge bilateral and regional agreements with like-minded countries.

More Bilateral or Regional
Free Trade Agreements?

Bilateral or regional free trade agreements are justified only in special cases. Israel, for political reasons, and Canada, for reasons of proximity and interdependence, are special cases. The European Community is also a special case on the latter score. President Reagan in his 1988 State of the Union address spoke of including Mexico in a North American accord. Mexico may also be a special case, but after that it is hard to see the U.S. Congress and the private sector in the United States going along with any other bilateral free trade agreements.

To put it bluntly, a succession of bilateral trade agreements is a recipe for RIBS—resentment, inefficiency, bureaucracy, and stupid signals. Resentment would prevail among outsiders. Inefficiency would be spawned by the fragmentation of markets. Bureaucratic nightmares would result for the government and for private firms trying to cope with the discrimination among countries. And stupid signals would be sent to those policy makers in developing countries who are proponents of markets and multilateralism. Lastly, other countries would protest if the United States tried to go beyond these special cases. After Canada, Israel, and maybe Mexico sometime in the next century, the options from a U.S. perspective are, or should be, spent.

And yet senior policy makers persist in pushing a strategy of bilateral agreements. Have they forgotten the lessons of history? A number of lessons can be learned from the experience of the 1930s, although today's political and economic circumstances make any extrapolation misleading. In the wake of the Smoot-Hawley tariff and subsequent retaliation, many countries tried to establish bilateral or regional agreements. But a proliferation of bilateral agreements is inconsistent with an expanding trading system.

Attempts in the interwar years to establish some predictability for trade, largely through discriminatory bilateral agreements, failed because the kind of certainty gained was illusory: the conclusion of the second or third discriminatory bilateral agreement necessarily disappoints expectations created by the first. (If, for example, the United States and Mexico were to sign an agreement covering auto parts, Canada would certainly have something to say about it.) Frictions, if not downright hostility, are bound to arise between the parties. Furthermore, if other countries were to follow the U.S. lead by trying to negotiate through bilateral agreements offering mutually incompatible privileges, predictability and stability would be destroyed for all countries.

While the experience of the 1930s may have limited relevance in today's world, it did demonstrate that discriminatory bilateral agreements cannot combine to form a globally consistent, stable system of national trade policies. Such a system requires effective equality of rights and obligations among countries, which can only be ensured by general acceptance of the principle of nondiscrimination embodied in most favored nation treatment. This principle mobilizes large nations to support the aspiration of small ones to be treated equally. In no other way can the sovereign equality of nations that differ enormously in size and power be realized, or even approximated.

Bilateral or like-minded groupings are an inferior alternative when compared with multilateral liberalization on a nondiscriminatory basis. Inevitably, some countries will be left out. How will they be chosen and who will decide? In the United States, Congress will have to play a role. Consider how members of Congress will be whipsawed by country interests and, disaggregating further, by sectoral interests. Legislative action in the United States on separate agreements also opens up the possibility that trade will be used as a weapon of foreign policy against countries that are not following in lockstep on recent foreign policy initiatives of the United States. How will domestic U.S. trade laws be interpreted or revised vis-à-vis nonmembers? Some legislators, pressed by special interests, may seek to discriminate in the application of domestic law.

All of this would raise trade policy from "low-level" to "high-level" foreign policy. James A. Baker III, the U.S. secretary of state and an earlier proponent of bilateral agreements, would end up spending more time on the balance of trade, leaving him less time to spend on the balance of terror. That would be a gross misallocation of resources. Equally important, the trade officials would be diverted from actively pursuing the Uruguay Round to time-consuming pursuit of bilateral alternatives.

Bilateral or like-minded agreements also will smack of colonialism to left-of-center politicians in many developing countries. Even for countries given preferential treatment, such an arrangement would add fuel to domestic political battles, to say nothing of the domestic political battles in countries discriminated against. This would certainly frustrate one of the objectives of the Uruguay Round, which is to integrate the developing countries more fully into the trading system.

The United States, Japan, and the European Community, the major pillars of the trading system, cannot afford to be in rival blocs. Western cooperation remains important for strategic and security reasons and must not be undermined. The best message of alliance cohesion the Western nations can send to Eastern bloc nations is a flourishing, unified, nondiscriminatory trading system. A fragmented trading system with friction and discrimination would send precisely the wrong signal.

In short, the arguments against regional agreements or a series of bilateral agreements are both political and economic. Politically, the essence of these agreements is that you play favorites, and that creates foreign policy problems with those that are discriminated against. If pursued, a misguided bilateral or regional strategy could alter the political contours of the alliance. Domestic political problems are also created. The U.S. Congress will be under pressure to withdraw trade preferences or withhold further liberalization if countries are deemed to be acting inconsistently with U.S. foreign policy objectives or if important domestic sectors are suffering increased competition from the country involved.

Most members of the U.S. Congress would prefer not to get involved in such micro management of trade and foreign policy initiatives. When they do, they find themselves whipsawed by differing interests. Frankly, the U.S. Congress probably does not have the time, resources, or political will to review, oversee, and legislate a series of bilateral or regional agreements with all of the attendant political pressures that they entail.

Notwithstanding these arguments against negotiating a series of bilateral or regional trade agreements, policy makers persist in proposing a bilateral agreement with Japan. The proposals are based either on false premises or on a misreading of the potential gains by paying insufficient attention to the negative consequences. A detailed examination of these proposals will serve to point out the problems and expose the limitations of a bilateral approach.

Arguments for and Drawbacks of a U.S.–Japan Bilateral Trade Agreement

Proponents of a bilateral trade agreement with Japan cite the corrosive effect that bilateral disputes have had on the U.S.–Japan relationship and the ineffectiveness of the piecemeal approach to solving disputes. But without internal reforms of the trade policy process in the United States to establish priorities and to give trade issues the greater attention they deserve, it is hard to see how a bilateral agreement with Japan would overcome these difficulties. And why should the United States assume that on the contentious issues (e.g., agriculture, construction, etc.) Japan would be any more able or willing to accede to American demands in the context of a negotiation to establish a bilateral free trade agreement? Wouldn't multilateral, not bilateral, pressure be more effective and more palatable politically within Japan? Furthermore, if somehow the United States succeeded in resolving festering disputes with Japan through a bilateral accord, the principle of unintended consequences would surely come into play, and one set of problems would be replaced by another as those countries discriminated against start to take policy actions to minimize the damage to them.

Another of the reasons cited for pursuing a bilateral accord with Japan is the European Community's effort to establish a Europe without borders by the end of 1992. The assumption is that the European Community will discriminate against outside interests as it liberalizes internally. But surely a bilateral approach to Japan would heighten the risk of a less outward oriented Europe and, as a number of European observers are now suggesting, could precipitate a push toward the Eastern bloc for markets and support. Further, given its past proclivity for regional agreements that infringe upon GATT obligations, the Community could also be expected to increase and strengthen its ties with the EFTA and other nonaffiliated countries.

The United States and Japan should welcome the 1992 effort but concert together and in the GATT to ensure maximum outward liberalization. The completion of the internal market should stimulate European growth and employment and thus trade with the rest of the world. Further, Europe 1992 is a good antidote to the overreaction of the American public about the coming "Pacific Century" and to the fears that have been spawned in some quarters. The Far East is the most dynamic region in the world today, but the Community's population is twice that of Japan and the four Asian NIEs combined, and Europe stands as the West's first line of defense against Eastern bloc aggression. The European Community has been a slumbering giant for some time, but now it is starting to wake up. The other giants, the United States and Japan, should not do anything to cause it to retreat. Nor can we afford to as far as defense and security are concerned.

That isn't to say there is nothing to be concerned about. Non-European interests should watch out to see: if Community directives call for a narrow application of reciprocity and establish European preferences to discriminate against outsiders; if the directives provide long phase-in times and safeguards for lagging sectors or for the poorer European countries; who negotiates regulatory standards for the Community, and on what basis outsiders can get mutual recognition of standards; if the multilateral talks are held hostage to the internal restructuring; how bilateral quotas on cars and textiles at the national level are converted to EC-wide quotas; and whether the directives are produced in a transparent way or behind closed doors with maximum uncertainty, which would have the same effect on firms outside as an increase in trade barriers.

It is important to ensure that the Community open up the ongoing process of completing the internal market to comments and criticism and to make certain that outsiders are not discriminated against. Outside interests should be more vigilant in monitoring what is going on in Brussels. If outside interests wait until the process has been completed, it will be too late. The Community's position will be set in concrete, leaving no room to maneuver at the Uruguay Round or elsewhere. A concerted policy to achieve transparency should be pursued in all appropriate forums such as the GATT, the OECD, and the Economic Summit.

A bilateral trade agreement between the United States and Japan would tie the hands of both countries' trade negotiators. The launch of the Uruguay Round at Punte del Este demonstrated the importance of coalition formation as a means for making progress. But coalitions shift from issue to issue. On market access to Japan, the United States might want to agree someday to join with the European Community to pressure Japan in a multilateral forum. But the United States and Japan may have to join together to ensure that the European Community does not use the 1992 effort as a means to discriminate against outside interests. And given the recent groundswell of protectionist sentiment in the United States, the day is coming when Japan and the European Community will want to join together to try to influence U.S. policy.

Isn't it better to retain the flexibility to form different coalitions and to use unilateral retaliatory measures to prod the process than to limit options by joining a bilateral agreement with another major pillar of the trading system? And from a domestic U.S. perspective, if other bilateral agreements are contemplated, it is not at all obvious which is the most appropriate partner. For example, on the one hand, Senator Max Baucus has proposed that the United States negotiate a bilateral agreement with Japan, while, on the other hand, Congress member Richard Gephardt has proposed that the European Community should be the object of U.S. bilateral initiatives. Who is going to decide and on what basis?

Granted, new options are needed in this highly pluralistic world to bring more pressure on the countries that are free riders and foot draggers. The preferred approach, however, should be a conditional MFN approach as was done with the Tokyo Round codes where only signatories to the code get the benefits from abiding by the additional discipline. Since the free riders and foot draggers will vary from issue to issue, this approach allows for greater flexibility. Especially in the new areas of services, investment, and intellectual property, a conditional MFN approach may be needed to avoid agreements reached on the basis of the lowest common denominator. But wouldn't negotiation of a far-reaching bilateral agreement complicate that course? Specific understandings with Japan on some of these issues could be brought into the Round to catalyze plurilateral arrangements that could gradually be extended.

Beyond these tactical issues, there are many practical reasons to reject a bilateral free trade agreement between the United States and Japan. The drawbacks are manifold. First, negotiation of a traditional free trade agreement covering tariffs and nontariff barriers or even including the new issues of services, intellectual property, and investment is too modest a goal. The most difficult problems the United States has with Japan, including the distribution system and cultural preferences, are not susceptible to negotiation by formula or by drafting new rules. Furthermore, the massive U.S. trade deficits with Japan, which have sparked protectionist sentiments, are largely due to macroeconomic phenomena. Are both countries prepared to talk about negotiations on monetary and fiscal policy? And where would this leave the G-7 process?

Second, the concessionary nature of negotiations requires that the United States "give up" something in the process. Will the United States, and in particular special interest groups and members of Congress, go along with dismantling import restraints on steel, autos, semiconductors, machine tools, textiles, and the other barriers that remain on Japanese exports to this country? What would the U.S. administration have to do to lay the groundwork for such an approach and then to see it through to a successful conclusion? Would the U.S. Congress be willing to set up an institutional apparatus for dispute settlement that would allow frictions with Japan to skirt U.S. trade remedy laws? Neither Israel nor Canada was able to obtain an exemption from existing U.S. trade remedy laws. Reverse the questions. What would Japan have to give up (rice?) and what would it take to make that acceptable to the farmers and the politicians who depend upon those votes?

Third, the U.S.–Canadian agreement is a good agreement, but it did not fully address many of the central difficulties of trade between the two countries, including subsidies, trade remedy actions, government procurement, and intellectual property. That agreement took almost two years to negotiate, and the talks came perilously close to collapse on several occasions. Before launching another bilateral agreement, would it not be better to wait to see how this one works out?

Fourth, both the United States and Japan have substantial

trade interests and business investments in other countries. Establishment of a free trade agreement would divert trade and investment, resulting in economic inefficiencies, which would raise consumer costs and alter sourcing patterns for firms with subsidiary operations in other countries. The extent of the net inefficiencies created would depend upon the balance between trade creation and trade diversion. Nonetheless, some consumers, affected multinational corporations, and third-country business interests would find cause to complain.

Fifth, even the onset of negotiations with Japan would cause other countries to change behavior and further erode the strengthening of the multilateral system. Other Asian countries would likely clamor for similar negotiations with either or both Japan and the United States, their major trading partners. The United States does not have the capability of conducting a series of bilateral agreements simultaneously, but could it afford to defer resolution of these requests until the U.S.–Japanese negotiations are completed? (And how is Canada affected and how does it respond?) How would America respond if the European Community moves to establish bilateral agreements of its own? And what would happen to the indebted countries of Latin America that depend on trade surpluses to service their debts but that would surely be harmed by the trade diversion entailed in bilateral agreements?

Finally, what would the consequences of failure be? The costs and consequences of failure need to be compared with the likely gains from any agreement. Can the gains be so great that risking the trading system as it now stands is worth taking the chance? As any negotiation of this type proceeds it occurs to the negotiators that the *status quo ante* is not the alternative in the wake of failed negotiations. Under those circumstances, negotiators are hard pressed to come up with an agreement, no matter how good or how workable. Can the world economy afford to take that risk?

The United States and Japan share the most important bilateral relationship in the world economy. Clearly, more needs to be done to manage the relationship. Both countries do have a significant number of complaints against the other. But a U.S.–Japan free trade agreement does not seem a realistic objective in the short run or an ideal objective in the long run. Instead, both countries should focus their efforts on reinvigorating multilateralism.

Conclusions

What should be done to reinvigorate multilateralism? The agenda of the Uruguay Round, as has already been said, contains the basic ingredients for an updated and strengthened multilateralism. The Round confronts the three faces of the GATT: the traditional face of the negotiating forum (concerning all tariffs and nontariff barriers in every sector of industry as well as the "new issues" of services, trade related intellectual property, and investment measures); the more familiar face of the GATT, the contract or agreement, to ensure that clearer rules of the road should be honored by a more timely and effective dispute settlement mechanism; and the new or potential but unformed face of GATT the institution, to build the third leg of the postwar tripod of multilateral institutions to foster improved coordinated management of global interdependence.

The chief instrument for systemic reform in the Uruguay Round is trade policy surveillance, i.e., regular analytic and evaluative reviews of a member country's trade related policies, *by a technically expert secretariat*—the microeconomic counterpart, in effect, to the Fund's surveillance function. The components of an effective trade policy surveillance would have to include an enhanced analytic capacity in the secretariat: a designated policy forum and, desirably, improved transparency of domestic trade policy-making procedures in member countries. The reviews would have to be distanced from the rule-based dispute settlement of the GATT or the scope of surveillance would be too narrow and the effectiveness of peer group pressure for policy adjustment and adaptation would be diminished or even nullified. By highlighting the impact of trade related policies on the country's domestic performance, on other countries' trade opportunities, and on the system as a whole, the surveillance mechanism would provide an avenue for both offsetting and preempting further serious erosion of the system.

The institution of a surveillance mechanism, more regular ministerial involvement, and improved coordination with the International Monetary Fund and the World Bank—the three issues covered by the FOGS negotiating group—would all raise the political profile of the GATT. This is an important feature of reform since the new protectionism in whatever form it is likely to take is neither transparent nor easily comprehended and thus evokes little public reaction—unlike an exchange-rate crisis or threat of a debtor's default. Strengthened coordination between the GATT and the financial institutions is not only desirable in itself (trade, debt, and exchange rates are hardly unrelated issues) but would also help reinforce the process of consultation *within* countries among trade, agriculture, and finance ministers, which is an essential feature of more coherent policy making in an increasingly interdependent world.

There is another aspect of systemic reform that is not included in the Uruguay Round negotiating agenda but which seems to be an essential ingredient for a reinvigorated multilateralism. It concerns the need for closer and more continuing relations between the GATT and the international business community. There is an irony that as business has become more global in orientation it has little or no contact with the global trade organization (unlike the situation for bankers and the international financial institutions, or the OECD with its Business and Industry Advisory Committee).

So the recipe for strengthened multilateralism is not a secret one: all the ingredients are known. A successful Uruguay Round would ensure that the beneficial effects of increased regional integration and higher noninflationary growth would far outweigh any trade-diversionary effects by spreading the benefits of greater liberalization and providing an early-warning mechanism for new manifestations of trade distortion.

But there is a more fundamental issue underlying the need for reinvigorated multilateralism in the present and foreseeable future. It lies in the link between trade and the broader economic picture. The current account imbalances may have diminished, but there is still a long way to go. One may debate the order of magnitude, the time path, or the precise policy mix, but what is not arguable is that elimination or substantial reduction of the U.S. current account deficit involves a very substantial deterioration in the current account position of other countries, with the heightened risk of protectionist pressures emanating from resistance to the painful process of structural change. In Europe this global adjustment process will coincide with another major force for structural change, the completion of the internal market. Clearly, the need to manage the process while sustaining world growth and improving the debt position of the Third World will call for improved policy coordination across the full range of policies. It will be very difficult, to say the least, to pull this off in the absence of a strengthened and credible GATT. So the stakes are extremely high.

Finally, it has been argued here that one hidden cost of the pursuit of bilateralism by the major world powers is the "crowding out" effect on multilateralism, i.e., the diversion of time, resources, and political commitment from the Uruguay Round. This "crowding out" is likely to be most serious in the case of the international public good aspects of the Round—the systemic strengthening of the GATT as an institution. So in that more fundamental aspect, the cost of U.S. bilateralism in a world where neither the EC nor Japan seems willing or able to assume the hegemonic role would have permanent and serious effects on the entire international economic system.

In sum, none of the alternatives to a renewed and reinforced GATT in the Uruguay Round is attractive. Of these, a series of bilateral initiatives is the most risky, destabilizing, and systemically damaging. The least bad may be a revival of the old idea of a "super GATT," i.e., plurilateral agreements housed in the GATT that could, over time, embrace the full multilateral agenda and GATT members. This would provide a real test of the management of global interdependence in a multipolar world. But it is unlikely to happen without U.S. leadership.

7

The Nature of American Global Leadership in the 1990s

DAVID M. ABSHIRE

How is the United States to maintain its leadership in the global economy in the 1990s? The answer to this question will depend upon what style of American leadership we select. Historically, we have seen a variety of styles of global leadership. First, there is leadership through the translation of military and economic power into direct leverage to accomplish certain objectives. Britain had such power during the Pax

DAVID M. ABSHIRE is president of the Center for Strategic and International Studies, an organization he cofounded in 1962. From 1983 to 1987 he served as the U.S. permanent representative on NATO's North Atlantic Council. Dr Abshire has served as a presidential appointee to three boards or commissions: the U.S. Board for International Broadcasting from 1974 to 1977; from 1973 to 1975, the Congressional Commission on the Organization of the Government for the Conduct of Foreign Policy; and from 1981 to 1983, the President's Foreign Intelligence Advisory Board. Dr. Abshire also has been an adjunct professor at the School of Foreign Service at Georgetown University, and has written numerous books and articles on international affairs. Dr. Abshire would like to express his appreciation to Jay Collins for his assistance in writing this chapter.

Britannica, mixing its maritime supremacy and capital financial strength. Another style is leadership through example: actions at home and abroad that build credibility and inspire others to follow. Lastly, there is leadership by persuasion through diplomacy and coalition building. This is the classical European approach, springing from Italian and French renaissance diplomatic practice.

In the postwar years, the United States has traditionally relied on superior power applying the leverage of its military might and security guarantee, its enormous market, and the strength of its currency to further its cause. Our leadership capability was reinforced by the credibility derived from the example of our domestic prosperity. Our successes commanded attention. The ability to act unilaterally, with or without the support of our allies, lessened the need for classical diplomacy, consensus, and compromise.

The nature of American global economic leadership in the 1990s will necessitate a different approach. In effect, we need a strategy to achieve a better balance among the three approaches. As our relative power position declines, persuasion, coalition building, and the art of the "indirect approach" become increasingly important.

In chapter 1, Raymond Vernon outlines the future global environment. By the year 2000 we will face a more multipolar world, with the United States, the Soviet Union, Japan, Europe, and China each creating gravitational fields. Power will increasingly be measured on multidimensional scales— military, economic, political, and technological—and today's superpowers will both be relatively less powerful.

Plainly, American leadership style will require a different mix of "carrots" and "sticks." American predominance in allied security relations, the international role of the dollar, and the size of its market make the United States the single most important actor in the international economic community. This generates considerable leverage. However, the pluralism of world economic power means that even the most important actor cannot have total dominance. Drastic depreciation of the dollar, a scaling back of U.S. commitments abroad, or the closure of its market will weaken U.S. influence still further.

Increased burden sharing in the Western Alliance in the 1990s must gradually lead to the sharing of decision-making power with our European and Japanese allies. America will have to cope with a multilateral system consisting of two huge economic power centers, Japan and the European Community (EC), on its transpacific and transatlantic flanks.

As we look ahead, the increased importance of diplomacy, persuasion, and the ability to function within multinational organizations will require the United States to build credibility abroad through its actions at home. The role of the United States as a global economic leader will diminish further unless we put our own house in order. It will not be possible to operate successfully from a position of debt, deficits, declining competitiveness, and a weakened educational system.

Furthermore, over the long run, the military strength of a nation cannot outlast its economic strength and productivity. Mikhail Gorbachev is a grand strategist who recognizes the connection between economic strength and military power. *Perestroika* is a result of this recognition.

We, too, must be grand strategists. As President Bush devises a strategy for renewed strength, the United States will need to address its domestic problems or it will lack the credibility to deal effectively in a global multilateral framework. As Henry Kissinger and Cyrus Vance said in a 1988 *Foreign Affairs* article, "Economic strength is . . . central to the way America is perceived by its friends and potential adversaries. U.S. political leadership in the world cannot be sustained if confidence in the American economy continues to be undermined by substantial trade and budget deficits." The United States has moved from producing nearly 50 percent of the world's goods and services after World War II, to about 20 percent today. In the last half of the 1980s we shifted from a solid position as a creditor nation to the world's leading debtor nation. Without indirect leadership through example, our ability to lead the world economy may falter.

Bold leadership in a crisis is common. Yet under conditions of relative domestic economic prosperity it is seldom seen. However, the problems of the twin deficits and American competitiveness will be infinitely more difficult to solve and solutions much less apparent if the present situation is allowed to deteriorate into a crisis. The danger is one of drift and inaction.

Changes in the Global System

The fundamental changes in the nature of the global system will have a direct impact on America's ability to lead in the twenty-first century. The diffusion of power makes unilateral actions by national actors less effective. The combined power of Europe as a single force, the enormous commercial strength of Japan, and the entrance of China and the newly industrialized countries into the global economic system diminish U.S. predominance. In relative terms, therefore, U.S. power has already declined. In fact, the very success of our postwar strategy made "relative" decline inevitable. Few today give America credit for the fact that our grand strategy of the 1950s worked brilliantly: witness the successful economic and political recovery and restoration of Europe and Japan, together with widespread economic development, especially in Asia.

Economic interdependence has also changed the way America relates to the rest of the world. To a certain degree, interdependence has made America vulnerable. We have lost what leaders and strategists seek to maintain—freedom of action. Desirable options in one area of economic concern are often precluded because of their effect in other areas, thus curtailing American flexibility and the ability to act independently. Moreover, the welfare of Americans can be threatened by the economic actions taken by other countries. "Internal" economic policies of developed and developing nations have a direct impact on the state of the global economy. The size of the Third World debt has called into question who has leverage over whom in certain situations. A debt moratorium by a number of debtor nations could set off a trade and economic crisis in our increasingly important economic relationship with the Third World.

While the domestic economic policies of our trading partners are beyond the scope of this chapter, it is important to note that successful rectification of enormous imbalances within the global trading system will not be possible without the implementation of rigorous corrective measures by our trading partners. While it may prove necessary to use substantial leverage of the U.S. market to achieve a more balanced liberal trading system, unilateral policy measures taken without prior consultation can backfire. America's macro- and microeconomic policies impact on and are impacted by global flows, trade, exchange rates, investments, growth, and inflation around the world. With increased interdependence and the growing complexity of the international economic system, coordination of macroeconomic policy adjustments among major trading partners is a prerequisite for the achievement of intended objectives.

Multiple Dimensions of Power and Leadership: A Strategic Approach

The nature of American leadership relates to the use of power and the creation of perceptions. Hence it is misguided to try to isolate different instruments of national leadership in terms of economic, political, and security components. In the 1990s economic leadership will depend on the accumulated totality of American power as it is perceived both at home and abroad. Since the beginning of the cold war, our economic leadership was enhanced by the fact that we were the defender of the free world, furnishing both the nuclear deterrent and forward-deployed conventional forces. One can therefore imagine the implications for U.S. leadership if the U.S. Congress were unilaterally to withdraw American forces from Europe, Japan, or South Korea.

The ability of the United States to provide global economic leadership will have tremendous implications for America's national security. In fact, the term "security" should be reinterpreted in the 1990s to include the economic dimension. The point is that global security involves what the Japanese call "comprehensive security." It involves protecting energy lifelines to our European and Pacific allies, technology cooperation, providing security assistance and debt relief, and of course staving off protectionism. It must include a more equitable sharing of the defense burden.

But here again the need is for a creative and reformist approach to defense and alliance challenges. In the 1950s the United States and its allies resorted to an overly nuclearized strategy due to the economic strain of an adequate conventional defense. That strategy, logical in an era of nuclear superiority, was based on the first use of nuclear weapons in order to stop a conventional attack. Such a strategy will become increasingly questionable in the 1990s. We need to rebalance the nuclear and conventional elements of our strategy in the 1990s, but in such a way as to achieve better return on our defense investment.

In an age of economic constraints, the reform of our overall strategy offers opportunities for developing a comprehensive defense investment strategy, Atlantic and Pacific, which can put an end to gross inefficiencies and the current misapplication of resources. At present, the United States and its allies invest more in security than the Warsaw Pact but have a less productive military output. Some forty armies, navies, and air forces in our alliance structure all manage separate budgets that place their own parochial needs and priorities first. This is further compounded by Atlantic and Pacific economic nationalism, weapons duplication, and lack of commonalities. The Warsaw Pact, on the other hand, starts with a given strategy, an operational concept, and enforced armaments cooperation. Our defense investment must be derived from a conceptual framework, from the top down. Many of our present problems could be solved if our defense investment were guided by an overarching strategy. The current crisis in our defense budget gives us an opportunity to move to create such a strategy.

Moving beyond defense strategy, the United States must build economic strength, and then harmonize it into a comprehensive strategy in a way that multiplies rather than divides that strength. Without such a strategy, we jeopardize not only our relative economic position in the world but our ability to finance the necessary military force. As we begin the 1990s, America faces a stringent reevaluation of its economic power-projection capability and its ability to honor global commitments with limited resources. This agonizing reappraisal of the mismatch between resources and commitments in different areas must take place simultaneously with the shoring up of our domestic economic position and the development of our economic strategy. Rarely have Americans thought in terms of a strategy for limited resources in the economic as well as the military field.

In the 1990s, American global economic leadership must be based on a sound strategy that seeks to minimize vulnerabilities and restore strength. U.S. strategy must seek to create the kind of economic environment we want, and this involves setting clear objectives and priorities. Rather than being guided by the latest political whim or the rising strength of a special interest group, policy should be guided by long-term strategic objectives. The application of such a long-term strategy involves consistency. Any economic strategy for America must integrate and interrelate trade policy, Third World debt policy, exchange rate policy, multilateral cooperation, and domestic economic restoration. This total strategy must be communicated to Congress to build coalition strength around it.

The failure of the United States to provide leadership through the restoration of its economic position at home and the elimination of global economic vulnerabilities, such as the Third World debt problem, could result in an economic crisis with devastating implications for the entire world. Such a crisis might result from a variety of scenarios, but let us look at one that is of particular concern. In the event of a global economic system characterized by regional trade and security blocs, the glue of the cold war that held the West together against a perceived threat in the 1950s and 1960s could dissipate. This could happen at the time that the Communist East, like the once centralized Ottoman Empire, itself begins to dismember in an explosive way.

Ironically, we would have the crises of communism and capitalism at the same time. The failure of communism and the nationalities problem facing the Soviets, combined with Gorbachev's radical attempts to restructure, could produce a leadership and governance crisis leading to unpredictable behavior by the Soviets and great uncertainties for the West. This would be especially dangerous if the Eastern European countries began to unravel and to pull away, followed by a Soviet military reaction. A sound and unified security system for the West becomes all the more important in such an unstable environment. Otherwise, we could return to the miscalculations and uncertain alliance commitments that brought about World War I. Clearly, in an age of mercantilism and protectionism, it would be extremely difficult to maintain a tight, cohesive alliance framework.

Domestic Economic Restoration

The eyes of the world are on America. Few understand the international consequences and the national security consequences of domestic economic policy. Without a domestic economic policy that reflects the realities of the global economy, we will damage not only ourselves, but the entire economic system, and eventually allied security. As a leader in the international economic community, we cannot ignore the international implications of our actions; some of our economic competitors no longer watch America with a desire to learn from our successes, as in the past. Instead they look with anxiety, hoping that the failure of America to solve its own economic problems will not lead to their own demise.

In shoring up the U.S. economic foundation, the first step

must be to restore our international payments position. The United States is a nation swimming in debt, with astronomical trade and budget deficits. The U.S. now pays more interest and dividends to foreigners than it earns from them. Not only are we borrowing to finance our trade deficit, but we are borrowing to pay interest on our debt. The size of future deficits will depend upon the joint actions by the legislative and executive branches. In the winter 1988/89 *Foreign Affairs*, C. Michael Aho and Marc Levinson write, "The sooner U.S. budget deficits are brought under control, the smaller the debt service requirements will be in the future and the sooner America will again project an image as the world's economic leader."

Adopting a rosy scenario and just muddling through presents great risks for the United States. If the flexible freeze fails and we have a recession, the steps that would be remedies now, such as dramatic budget reductions, could make the crisis worse.

If the United States takes responsible steps on the budget, we will not have the difficulty President Reagan had in his second term of getting allied cooperation in promoting domestic demand-driven growth. Pressure for protectionism, as huge cuts are taken in the current accounts of surplus countries, will be eased only by macroeconomic policies that encourage strong growth rates in order to offset the aggregate effect of deteriorating trade surpluses. Globally, the burden of controlling inflation and interest rates cannot be left to monetary policy alone. Fiscal policy must be controlled as well.

The U.S. budget deficit, together with the low rate of private savings, has created a dependence on foreign capital that affects the domestic economy in a variety of ways. Capital inflows have allowed growth in public and private consumption to exceed the growth in domestic production. One cannot assess the impact on the U.S. economy of foreign capital without differentiating between foreign direct investment (FDI) and holdings of highly liquid assets, especially those used to finance America's debt.

The first, FDI, results in many benefits to the economy, including job creation and greater competitiveness. This is evident from the degree to which state and local governments compete to attract it. For example, over thirty-five states have offices in Tokyo actively pursuing Japanese investors. Restrictions on FDI could trigger a run on the dollar; our focus, therefore, should not be on restricting private foreign investment but on opening up opportunities for Americans to invest abroad as freely as foreigners invest here. For national security reasons the maintenance of a strong industrial base in the United States is essential. In nonsensitive areas where U.S. capital is insufficient, foreign capital from allies should be welcomed, not barred from making up the shortfall.

On the other hand, dependence on foreign capital for deficit funding and the high degree of liquidity of these assets create financial vulnerability. For example, what would happen if Japanese institutional investors suddenly lost confidence in the dollar's stability? The immediate impact on interest rates and global confidence in the dollar would be tragic. Critics of this scenario say that the Japanese have nowhere else to go. However, with the planned integration of Europe by 1992, we are already seeing a measured diversification by the Japanese into European assets.

The United States has done little to correct the consumer orientation of our economy and promote greater savings. Rather than borrowing to invest in high-yield, long-term activities, such as developing new technology or processes, we borrow to consume. This present-day consumption beyond our means is being subsidized by foreigners and will have to be paid back through reduced consumption in the future.

With the growing recognition of this problem, it is odd that our current tax law promotes consumption, and reduces savings and long-term investments. The absence of inflation adjustment for capital gains, interest, and depreciation; the disallowance of all interest and dividend deductibility; and the often double taxation of dividends actually discourage long-term investments. During the Reagan administration, one of the primary economic goals was to control inflation. In the future, however, President Bush must move beyond inflation control to develop a more balanced relationship among spending, production, and savings.

The second of the twin deficits, in trade, will remain an urgent priority for the Bush administration. We must begin at home with a domestic economic policy that encourages exports and eases the burden of trade adjustment. The Trade Act of 1988 should be evaluated with this principal objective in mind. Consistency of effort across the spectrum means that the United States must ensure that budget cuts do not impair our ability to improve U.S. export performance. For example, funding for the Export-Import Bank ought to be increased rather than cut.

The United States must take decisive action to lower the trade deficit, while remembering that the trade imbalance has become a structural problem, both internally and externally. The economies of most surplus countries have been adjusted toward export orientation while American companies have pulled out of markets, reorienting toward imports. In fact, the enormous imbalances within the global economy that have taken some five years to create may take even longer to correct.

As thirty-three economists from thirteen countries said in December of 1987, protectionism

would be the height of folly for the U.S. just as its competitive position is improving and it seeks a $150–$200 billion gain in its trade balance, because it would surely trigger retaliation from countries that are both prospering less than America and which now must accept large declines in their trade positions.

We need a clear strategy to achieve the adjustment necessary to eliminate the structural economic imbalances while continuing to control our inflation, maintain growth, and avoid protectionism. Reagan often abdicated White House leadership on trade issues. Bush must restore executive leadership on trade policy, and policies must be built around a coalition based on "export politics." If the president is going to use trade sanctions, they must be used only in retaliation and with the objective of strengthening compliance with the international trading system. Historically, the real intent of sanctions has been to close markets rather than to open them.

While Americans are quick to emphasize the importance of free trade and open markets, U.S. trade policies often leave little room to maneuver. The Reagan administration imposed new or tighter restrictions on textiles, sugar, semiconductors, autos, steel, machine tools, lumber, etc. Gary Hufbauer, a Georgetown University U.S. trade expert, estimates that the proportion of U.S. imports affected by trade barriers rose from 12 percent in 1970 to 23 percent in 1989. He calculates that the cost to the U.S. consumer of these import restraints was $81 billion in 1989, up from $16 billion in 1970. It is important to realize that import relief tends to be permanent. The United States must avoid any further use of voluntary restraint arrangements, which hurt consumers, give no incentive to U.S. companies to adjust, and *result in windfall profits* to foreign companies due to price increases. Lowering the current level of restrictions can be used not only as an example of American leadership, but also as leverage to extract comparable reductions from other trading partners.

But our ability to set an example as a nation that supports the principles of a free trade system will be greatly affected by the hardships of those who suffer from the adverse effects of a free trade system. There were some 11 million displaced American workers between 1981 and 1986. By aiding adjustment for those who have been displaced by international trade, we would considerably reduce political pressures for protectionism. We must deal effectively with the problem of worker adjustment or we will lose the flexibility necessary to maintain competitiveness in a rapidly changing global economic environment. The United States, more so than most countries in the Organization for Economic Cooperation and Development (OECD), lacks an adequate adjustment program that would deal with workers who suffer from the adverse effects of free trade.

Competitiveness

Although the United States has recently made progress on competitiveness, we have a long way to go in compensating for the lag in the growth of labor productivity and capital formation. Insufficient capital and research and development (R&D) investments, poor labor-management relations, excessive government regulation, and the predominance of short-term thinking have resulted in a weakened competitive position. While some companies have moved to improve their competitiveness and productivity by emphasizing a "total quality approach" as well as better labor-management relations, many have not made adequate progress.

Competitiveness involves technological innovation, attention to quality, productivity growth, and educated workers. According to a presidential commission, competitiveness must at the same time involve higher real income for American citizens. Our comparatively low level of R&D (resulting from the high cost of capital) and our feeble productivity growth (0.6 percent in the 1970s and 0.4 percent in the 1980s) are two of the most blatant problems.

The "soft" side of competitiveness and productivity is often more important than we realize (i.e., quality control, organization of resources, labor-management relations). For example, a study done by Peter Morici in 1984 showed a $2,000 Japanese cost advantage in a 1983 subcompact car. Twenty-three percent of this advantage resulted from lower wages and production techniques, 63 percent from management systems, and 8 percent from better labor-management relations.

Greater investment in human resources would increase our competitiveness and help restore our industrial strength. As we look at our competitive position, we must ask ourselves why Japan, with half the population of the United States, has more scientists and engineers. Why, on average, does Japan invest twice as much capital per worker as does the United States? As a percent of gross national product (GNP), Japan invests much more in manufacturing plants and equipment than the United States does. Why has the United States not given education the priority it needs? America's children suffer from high illiteracy rates and relatively poor science and math skills.

Education is directly related to a nation's ability to compete. The Commission of Excellence in Education wrote, in *A Nation at Risk,* of our deteriorating educational foundation. Thirteen percent of our seventeen-year-olds are functionally illiterate. The illiteracy rate among minorities is 40 percent, and approximately 3,000 students drop out of high school every day. If America is to lead the world in the next century, it must act immediately to rectify and improve our educational system. Making education a budgetary priority will have a long-term payoff for the strength of the U.S. economy.

Organizing to Lead

Leadership, strategy, and organization are the three sides of a triangle that, if effectively combined, create national strength. This applies in both the economic and security areas. Yet the problem is that by and large the Washington government, on and off Capitol Hill, is compartmentalized rather than integrative, reactive rather than anticipatory. Washington is too often divided and subdivided within itself. Hence, even when strong personal leadership is present, it is difficult to develop a strategy for truly effective long-term action.

U.S. economic leadership cannot be effective without better organization and economic coordination at home. Economic policy formulation must take into consideration the crossovers and interrelationships between debt and trade, capital flows and merchandise flows, domestic policy and international economic policy. The compartmentalization and lack of adequate policy integration have convinced me that we ought to rethink how we do business in the Washington economic arena.

One of the constraints on America's ability to formulate and execute economic policy is the diffusion of power throughout the government. The fractionalization and balkanization of economic policy throughout the executive and legislative branches of government preclude a coherent strategy. Every department, agency, and committee relating to economics has its own approach. All too often these approaches are implemented independently. This balkanization is reflected in our inability to present an integrated and united front when negotiating with our trading partners on multiple issues.

In Congress, the decline of bipartisanship, the decentralization of power, the rise of single issue groups, and the tendency to make policy by amendment all detract from our ability to think and act strategically in the economic arena. One of the most glaring examples is the Omnibus Trade Bill that was worked on by a cumbersome Senate-House committee during 1987 and finally passed in 1988. The new law, even in its final form, was far from a coherent piece of legislation. Yet one should not expect coherence out of legislation written in a piecemeal fashion by hundreds of staffers in both the House and Senate. Literally hundreds of amendments were added to the dozens of separate bills, making up a document of over a thousand pages.

One of the remedies that I have endorsed, as the result of a transition of government study that I cochaired with Robert Hunter at the Center for Strategic and International Studies (CSIS), is that there ought to be an assistant to the president for international economic policy coordination. I know that such a proposal frequently gives ex-leaders of the Treasury Department, and certainly a recent Federal Reserve chair, Paul Volcker, deep concern. The primary criticism of such an idea is that economic policy might be sacrificed to foreign policy. However, the assistant's role should not be one of determining monetary policy, any more than the national security advisor can or should command the joint chiefs of staff. Such an individual, like the national security advisor in the security arena, would break down the interagency compartments and ensure coordination and consistency of effort across the economic board.

The CSIS transition report also concluded that the president must personally take the lead in economic policy development. While some have suggested that President Reagan took a less than keen interest in economic policy, President Bush has shown that he plans to play a central role in economic policy formulation. Ultimately, the president must take the lead in international trade if he is going to succeed in keeping the lightning rod of protectionism away from the Congress.

The president must develop an economic strategy and make it understood and endorsed through a partnership with Congress—all this early in the administration. Otherwise the window of opportunity may close, and deep divisions within the government would again come to the forefront. Despite the problems we face, confidence can be built and maintained as long as the president has a clear sense of direction and strong strategic priorities. A comprehensive strategy does not mean doing everything at once; it means formulating priorities but also seeing them in an overall framework.

Over the next decade there are two areas where policy coordination and long-term integration will be essential: Europe and Japan. In order to give these two areas the necessary priority, U.S. government needs to create two cabinet councils. The first should integrate and interrelate the elements in our various relations with Japan, and the second should do the same with the European Community. Both of these councils should have joint meetings with their Japanese and EC counterparts. A similar suggestion was put forward by Peter Ludlow with regard to the European Community. These councils would go beyond economic considerations to a range of security and political matters. The integrative work of the U.S. cabinet council would also be enormously helpful in conveying a sense of overall strategy to the Congress.

Another suggestion that I have recommended elsewhere is that the president should appoint a presidential counselor for the integration of long-range planning in both the security and economic fields. Only President Eisenhower had the wise judgment to keep long-range policy free of day-to-day crisis management, and his wisdom should be readopted and up-graded. As well as integrating the various government planning bodies scattered throughout the multitude of departments and agencies, the counselor would also perform the necessary contingency planning, which is so often neglected.

Multinational Forums and International Institutions

As any unilateral action by the United States grows less effective, the multilateral approach to global problems will become more important. Multilateral consultative organizations and forums, such as the General Agreement on Tariffs and Trade (GATT), the World Bank, the International Monetary Fund (IMF), G-7, Summit-7, and GATT negotiation, provide excellent frameworks for seeking greater cooperation on a broad range of issues. Yet this will require America to adopt a different style, involving greater finesse, diplomacy, and increased complexity. Through the greater involvement of international forums, we could de-Americanize many problems that are traditionally seen as America's responsibility.

GATT

In order to maintain credibility in the trade arena, the president should put his political capital behind making the Uruguay trade round a complete success. We must aim at updating and broadening the mandate of the General Agreement on Tariffs and Trade. The GATT has been extremely successful in accomplishing its original purpose—the reduction of worldwide tariffs to relatively low levels. Today, however, the barriers that inhibit international trade are no longer tariffs, but trade barriers such as quotas and voluntary export restraints.

We need to strengthen the GATT as an institution, improving mechanisms for the settlement of disputes and developing a surveillance procedure for periodic reviews of trade policies.

It needs to take bold steps to deal with agriculture, which has until now been only imperfectly covered by GATT. Agricultural subsidies and restrictions have created global economic imbalances and staggering surpluses that cost consumers billions of dollars a year.

GATT, in its conception forty years ago, did not need the capability to deal with such problems as intellectual property rights and the service industries. Now, however, unless it can deal successfully with these areas it will lose the credibility it so badly needs. The 1982 Greenberg study on GATT and the service industry led Ambassador William Brock, then U.S. trade representative, to push to have the important issue placed on the GATT agenda. In the 1990s, without a broader mandate and greater authority, GATT will become increasingly irrelevant.

The Uruguay Round ought to strive for a package deal that would involve compromises and concessions from all parties concerned. In addition to the liberalization of agriculture, such a deal might include a revised and reinforced safeguard clause, a gradual phasing out of the Multifiber Agreement (bringing it into compliance with GATT rules), and tighter discipline on quota restrictions, present and future. Furthermore, developing countries would have to agree to new limitations on the use of trade restrictions for balance-of-payments reasons.

A U.S. commitment to make the Uruguay Round a success will mean little unless the Europeans are willing to look beyond their own internal negotiations and dedicate themselves to making GATT work. While European officials say that 1992 will stay within GATT rules, many critical areas such as financial services are not currently covered by GATT. Unless they are carefully managed, European directives involving the harmonization of standards, new rules of origin, reciprocity, and the transfer of national quantitative restrictions to the EC level could become the building blocks of a fortress Europe.

Recent progress in GATT gives cause for hope. Dispute resolution panels have cut decision time from several years to six months. GATT handled as many complaints in the two-year period 1987–1989 as it did in its previous thirty-nine years of existence. Most importantly, many countries are beginning to abide by GATT rulings. In 1988, for example, Japan accepted a negative GATT ruling on twelve groups of food products, despite domestic political difficulties. Tokyo has even filed its own GATT complaint, something that had been avoided by the Japanese government until recently.

If GATT is to continue to make progress in dealing effectively with the many challenges that lie ahead, it may well need an executive committee along with a new injection of financial resources. Looking ahead to the year 2000, however, the GATT in current form will not be enough to cope with the increasingly complex range of trade, technology, and investment related issues. The CSIS project on the future global trading system proposes drawing up a detailed blueprint for an international trade and investment organization that would manage and coordinate the various multilateral, regional, and bilateral trade relationships that are currently evolving.

In this same CSIS study, Ambassador Ernest Preeg suggests that the United States pursue a "three-convergent-track" approach to trade policy: multilateral negotiations through GATT; regional arrangements; and bilateral negotiations. According to the study:

A successful Uruguay Round, together with careful management of the regional momentum for trade liberalization and bilateral trade policy objectives, should set the stage for more definitive movement toward a predominantly multilateral framework for trade and investment relations by the end of the 1990s.

The study concludes that the recent movements on regional and bilateral agreements will continue into the 1990s. Thus it is of vital importance that we reconcile and make mutually supportive the various trade policy tracks.

The positive implications of lowering trade barriers among major regional trading partners cannot be disputed. It is estimated that the Canadian Free Trade Agreement will result in a 3 percent rise in Canadian GNP and a 1 percent rise in U.S. GNP. This has been accomplished without reducing market access to outsiders. Thus regional agreements, if done properly, can reinforce the multilateral liberal trade regime. However, the ramifications of regional arrangements that break down barriers from within, only to construct a fortress around the perimeter, give cause for deep concern.

The fear of such fortresses in Europe and North America has driven Japan and others to talk of a yen bloc. While Japan and other Asian surplus countries could hardly afford to sacrifice the European market in place of a stronger Asian market, some believe that an Asian bloc would create enough leverage to ensure that Europe does not build a protectionist wall. The growing predominance of Japan and the strength of the yen in Asia have made such a bloc a distinct possibility. Seventy percent of Japanese economic aid, which reached $10 billion in 1988, is concentrated in Asia. Meanwhile, Japanese trade with Indonesia, Malaysia, the Philippines, and Thailand went from $3.2 billion in 1970 to $76.1 billion in 1987. During this same period American trade with these countries only grew from $4 billion to $17.8 billion. At the same time, however, Japan's neighbors do not want their economics dominated by Japanese economic interests.

If the Uruguay Round is not a success, the trading system may well deteriorate into a series of inward-looking regional and bilateral agreements. Furthermore, trade arrangements, which undercut the most favored nation principle, could jeopardize the multilateral system. A trading system based on outwardly protectionist trading blocs would be very complex, involve great inconsistencies, require more attention to varying regulations, and have a daunting effect on the global flow of goods, services, and capital.

Inward oriented trading blocs could also have an effect on the solidarity of Western security. Allied unity would be lost, and Moscow could take advantage of divisions within the alliance system. A fortress Europe, for example, could quickly lead to the deterioration of America's willingness to maintain its commitment to European security. Protectionism in the European Community would very likely lead to a congressional move toward troop withdrawals.

The G-7 and Exchange Rate Stability

Another area where the United States must continue to play a leadership role in a multilateral forum is exchange rate stability. Relative exchange rate stability is based on fundamental economic determinants and is the foundation on which the global trading system must stand; stability at unrealistic rates disrupts trade and distorts the global trading system.

The G-7 should move beyond the "indicators" approach of the 1986 Tokyo Summit and the "reference ranges" of the February 1987 Louvre Accord to a system of more formal target zones. These "zones," however, must be at a level that will result in a rectification of current account imbalances. In addition, exchange rate objectives set by policy makers have little meaning unless multilateral economic policy adjustments are coordinated.

American policy makers must act to restore credibility abroad through certain domestic fiscal and monetary policies if any degree of dollar stability is to be maintained. Senator Bill Bradley has said that if the United States had to resolve its trade imbalance through a reduction in imports, it would have to reduce the domestic demand equivalent of the entire Mexican economy. Thus surplus countries must maintain growth if the United States is to adjust through export expansion rather than import reduction and if currency markets are to remain stable.

The understanding reached at the Louvre Accord in 1987 has been criticized for sacrificing national flexibility in making internal economic policy. The British have not joined the European Monetary System, which seeks to regulate the volatility of European currencies, due to its implications for internal economic policy control. Yet without broad collective agreements among the G-7 on exchange rates and the implementation of domestic economic policies to support them, exchange rate volatility will continue to disrupt free trade.

International Financial Institutions and Debt

A CSIS conference on the presidential transition held in August of 1988 concluded that the debt crisis would be one of the most urgent problems facing American leaders in 1988. Most participants believed that the debt time bomb would have to explode before any bold action would become politically feasible. America and other OECD countries must embrace already existing international financial institutions if the Third World is ever going to be given a fighting chance.

Indebtedness and stagnation in developing countries threaten the entire economic order, and the problem is getting worse, not better. Between 1973 and 1985 the debt of less developed countries (LDCs) rose from $130.1 billion to $1 trillion. The solution to the debt problem and the economic development of the Third World will not take place without free trade. The efforts of the IMF and the World Bank to ensure that new capital and credit continue to flow to the Third World are of critical importance.

Third World debt has taken a serious toll on America's current account position. The United States has had to absorb an inordinate amount of the burden of providing a market for developing countries' goods. LDC debt-service burdens squeeze the amount of U.S. exports to developing countries. One estimate has shown that the sale of American goods to Latin America has been reduced by $20 billion a year due to the debt burden.

Especially in the case of Latin America, the political, social, economic, and security implications of a failure of America to play a leadership role in easing the debt burden are huge. Having paid $180 billion in interest on their $420 billion debt, Latin American countries are already beginning to face tremors in their political foundations. Annual interest from Latin American countries amounts to approximately $30 billion a year. In Argentina, Brazil, Peru, and other countries throughout the region, extremist parties are gaining strength, and the possibilities for military coups increase. As Mexico struggles with its exorbitant debt, social conditions continue to slide downward. For example, in the years 1982–1988, average purchasing power in Mexico dropped 40 percent. America's leadership will weigh heavily on the political and socioeconomic future of Latin America.

The flow of resources must be reversed so that they go into developing countries instead of out of them. Unfortunately, while the Third World faces a net capital outflow, commercial banks continue to look for ways to reduce their exposure. At the same time, even the IMF received net debt repayments of $1 billion in 1987. If commercial banks are seeking to lower their exposure and our international financial institutions continue to receive net funds, who will fund Third World growth?

The Brady Plan reflects the Bush administration's belief that the debt crisis is indeed a national security problem. While the initial preparation and coordination of the plan within the executive branch fall short of what might have been expected, the urgency of a major debt relief package is indisputable. At the time of this writing, the details of the plan have yet to be fleshed out. It is unclear, therefore, how the plan will deal with the problem of capital flight and what measures will be taken to ensure the necessary fundamental policy reforms in debtor countries so as to prevent such a crisis from recurring.

What is clear at this stage is that such a debt relief package will require greater financial resources for the IMF and the World Bank. It should be emphasized to the U.S. Congress and to our European and Japanese allies that in attempting to give relief to the Third World we must not cripple our international financial institutions.

Summit-7

Although the Summit-7 meetings are very different from the international institution meetings, they too provide a multilateral forum that could be put to more effective use. Present-day Summit-7 meetings have become largely ceremonial. Despite the movement to address broader security considerations, as at Williamsburg and Tokyo, there is much more room for improvement in the nature, scope, and depth of these meetings.

First, the so-called sherpas who prepare for the meetings are by themselves insufficient. At a minimum, the Summit-7 needs to have political directors who meet regularly from those nations' capitals to discuss broad economic and security cooperation. These directors should be reinforced by officials from the finance ministries and other agencies from the capitals, depending on the agendas of the meetings. Their mandate should be broad enough to allow them to talk about common concerns ranging from energy lifelines and Third World debt to security assistance and terrorism.

This strengthening of the Summit-7 would have numerous advantages. It would move the topics of the summits away from the crisis management of the moment to more long-range problems. It would force nations to consult in a multilateral forum on a regular basis, just like the Special Consultative Group or the High Level Group at NATO. As with NATO, once the framework is set up there is no excuse for not consulting. In addition, it would force the United States and others to have greater policy coordination within their own governments.

In the development and use of the various international forums and institutions it is essential that we have a sound, well-coordinated economic strategy. Without such a strategy the interrelationships between security and economics, Third World debt and development, and trade and technology will be overlooked. If we were to develop a strategy to make better use of the various international consultative mechanisms and coordinate their objectives, the payoffs would be tremendous. However, if we fail to develop an integrated approach, our credibility as a leader will be diminished and our policies will remain inconsistent and confusing to our allies.

Take for example the objective of strengthening the free trading system. GATT should no longer be forced to carry the entire burden when so many other forums can contribute directly or indirectly to the process. International financial institutions could promote growth in developing countries that enables them to import more, thus opening up markets for American products. Consequently, their role in trade promotion could be crucial. Paul Volcker has suggested that international financial institutions ought to be more concerned about trade: the World Bank should help with trade adjustment through sectoral and structural adjustment loans while the IMF might be well advised to do an assessment of the effects of protectionism.

Clearly, there ought to be some way to better relate and coordinate the efforts of the GATT, OECD, World Bank, and IMF. At a minimum, there ought to be greater linkage between these institutions at the ministerial level and below. This will require a political directive and should be placed on the summit agenda.

Another example of the need for policy coordination first at home, then abroad, is the issue of how GATT and international financial institutions, such as the World Bank and IMF, deal with nonmarket economies. The Soviets view entrance into these institutions largely as a political goal. With regard to the multilateral trading system, GATT is a set of legal commitments about market oriented access for exports, and the Soviets do not yet have a substantive basis for such commitments. In the case of financial institutions, without widespread access to data on Eastern economies and far greater transparency in the Soviet Union, there will be no conceivable way to integrate them into the West in a manner that does not jeopardize the system. On the other hand, should the Soviets move toward compliance with such a standard, the impact of market forces on the Soviet economy could only be positive, and the transformation of the Soviet empire no less than revolutionary. If done cautiously, we can engage Gorbachev constructively in the world economy.

Final Comments

As we analyze the course of American economic leadership, it is possible to identify two distinct attitudes toward the next millennium. The first discounts any fear about the future as long as we maintain our confidence and optimism. In contrast to Jimmy Carter, who cloaked himself in problems and articulated national malaise and limitations, Reagan shrugged off such limitations and restored the confidence and image of America. Thus, according to this view, President Bush must stay the course without fear of overly hyped economic vulnerabilities.

The second attitude views America's decline as inevitable. Eventually all great powers decline, it is believed, and the time has come to suffer the consequences of our global overstretch; the best we can do is to "manage our decline" in the hope of preventing a free fall. Retrenchment will be necessary to wall off our national strength, protecting our technology, industry, and our real estate. Those who take this view feel that it is time to scale back our global commitments and turn the international leadership of the world economy over to the next in line.

There is, however, a third view, quite different from the others. It involves acknowledging the vulnerabilities and potential for peril that could cause America's decline. Rather than papering over problems, it admits there are limitations. Yet this approach combines an optimism about the future with the assurance that the outcome is in our hands. With the proper leadership, strategy, and organizational mechanisms, we can restore national strength.

The third attitude also involves developing trade-offs, building coalitions within the government and among allies, and results in a totality that is greater than the sum of its parts. It means not just making the global economy work for us, but restoring national character at home and confidence in America abroad. It requires facing up to problems and turning them into opportunities for improvement. This approach will require flexibility, forward thinking, and new creativity. Ultimately, it means working within the global system rather than against it.

One often hears talk about how Japan is scheming to buy America. The fear of Japanese domination runs across the United States from Hawaii to Washington, D.C. Yet the talk in Tokyo is quite different. One hears, instead, a deep concern about the ability of the United States to rebuild its economy and the need for America to hold firmly to the reins of global leadership. There is no substitute!

Appendix

The Global Economy in the Year 2000: Driving Forces, Scenarios, and Implications

JAN V. DAUMAN

This appendix will offer a view of what the global economy may look like by the year 2000. The author recognizes that there is no certainty about the future. The only certainty is that surprises will happen. The best that can be hoped for is to consider alternatives, and assess the probability of their occurrence. This is especially true in the area of predicting global trends.

The world is becoming increasingly interdependent; problems are complex and global in nature and require complex global solutions. The last quarter of the present century is marked by increasing volatility. Straight-line forecasting or extrapolation is likely to be more misleading than at any time in

JAN V. DAUMAN is chief executive of the InterMatrix Group, an international consulting and business development firm he co-founded in 1973. Dr. Dauman's specialization is in globalization and other aspects of global strategy, including the formation and implementation of crossborder strategic alliances. He has been involved in European integration issues for over twenty years and is currently advising U.S. and Asian companies on Europe 1992. He has written and lectured widely on these topics.

the past. This complexity—the profusion of elements to be considered and the speed at which they change—makes most prognostications inaccurate almost the moment they are pronounced. Yet to make policy, one should have set assumptions about the future on which to base recommendations.

The United States cannot afford to guess wrong about the course of world events. America's pivotal position in geopolitics and the global economy places upon U.S. policy makers the responsibility to develop a workable vision of the future: one that is *comprehensive,* to take into account the diversity of influences that shape the world; *creative,* to go beyond conventional wisdom in unconventional times; and, most of all, *dynamic,* to respond to the change that is the only reliable constant.

The purpose of this appendix is to help produce such a vision, and to suggest the place of the United States in the picture. To that end, the following methodology is proposed:

- Develop a common view of how the world is shaped—the *driving forces* that have brought global society to its current state.
- Use these forces to construct *scenarios,* or alternative pictures, of the way the world might be shaped in the future.
- Assess the probability of occurrence of each scenario and focus on the most likely or "base case."
- Analyze the base case scenario to identify the *issues* that are likely to be of concern to society as a whole in the year 2000 and beyond.
- Establish a "snapshot" of key events in the year 2000, illustrating the trends and developments in the base case scenario.
- Derive the *implications* for the United States of the world described by these forces, scenarios, and issues.

Once a workable world view has been developed, we can then move ahead with the task of recommending policy responses to the challenges presented. Given the high level of volatility, the responses need to be sufficiently robust to withstand a range of plausible outcomes.

Unless a consistent set of assumptions is made explicit,

agreed, communicated, and used by decision makers, there is a high risk of different strategies being formulated by different groups being based on varying, sometimes unrealistic, and often conflicting assumptions.

The Path to the Year 2000: How We Got There from Here

Driving Forces

What causes the various institutions of human beings—countries, companies, multinational organizations—to behave as they do? What motivating factors lie behind the decisions that ultimately determine the course of world events? The answers are critical to understanding the present and predicting the future.

The following list of driving forces represents views gathered from a variety of experts from across the political, sociological, and geographical spectrum and refined over the past two decades. It is not meant to be a checklist of concerns that all nations should share; rather, it is meant to pick out certain seemingly universal forces that are likely to continue to drive global events through the year 2000.

- *Pulls to interdependence.* The vast investments, beyond the treasuries of many nation states and companies, needed for high-technology research and development (R&D); the growth in mass communications; the convergence of consumer taste; the demands of economies of scale.
- *Monetary flows/exchange rates.* Changing the shape of the global economy; impacting capital investment and consumer savings; reflecting balance of payment and trade credits and deficits.
- *Technology/information.* Widespread access to both is continuing to impact competitiveness, diminish the importance of political boundaries, make the world "smaller," and accelerate the cycle of global events.

- *Energy.* The price of oil is a key determinant of the nature and pace of economic development, and stability of supply is a major influence on world peace.
- *Regionalism.* Economic nationalism is giving way to economic regionalism as countries have to combine economies of scale with protectionism to survive.
- *Debt.* Third World indebtedness continues to be one of the major challenges to the world financial system, and affects markets and stability in the indebted countries.
- *Population/demographics.* Birth rates, aging trends, and the size and prosperity of the work force affect the very nature of a government's relationship with its citizenry and drive markets and competitiveness.
- *Leadership.* The combination of timely innovation and personal commitment has been shown most recently by Ronald Reagan and Mikhail Gorbachev, Lord Cockfield (architect of "Europe 1992") and Mrs. Thatcher. Conversely, lack of leadership retards the progress of international initiatives such as the fight against trade protectionism and debt.
- *Growth.* The goal of economic growth and political maturity and the ability to achieve that goal will determine the success of the USSR's *perestroika,* the U.S. administration's ability to reduce the twin deficits, the recovery of Latin America.
- *Ideology.* The failure of liberalism of the 1960s and the return to "old fashioned" or fundamentalist beliefs have led to the successful appeal of Reaganism and Thatcherism and the rise of religious fundamentalism worldwide.
- *Military-Industrial complex.* The conventional vs. nuclear weapons debate remains the backdrop for modern superpower politics. Reduction in power bloc military spending will have significant economic impacts.
- *Environment.* The rise of "Green" politics is connected to the perception that concern for the environment is a legitimate brake on economic development "at all costs."
- *Weather.* Climate and natural disasters continue to be natural checks and balances on economic development.

The importance of understanding driving forces is under-scored by comparing some of the basic facts about the world economy today with, say, the 1950s. As Table 1 shows, albeit in a simplified, cryptic form, today's world is very different across all dimensions. Yet many of the institutions and processes built to deal with the critical issues have not changed with equivalent speed, posing the inevitable question about their capacity to be effective. The answer to this question is itself a fundamental driving force; indeed, some would argue that it is the single most important determinant of what will actually happen in the decade to come.

Views of the World in the Year 2000: Alternative Scenarios

Just as one set of facts can be used to support very different conclusions, so can a set of causal factors produce very different outcomes. Predictions of the future often go wrong because they hinge on one and only one possible outcome, thus dramatically lowering the chances of accuracy—and of developing appropriate strategies for coping with future events.

A more dynamic, and ultimately more realistic, approach involves developing several possible outcomes. The need is to develop and assess the probability of occurrence of the more likely scenarios. Once these likelihoods have been established, the most likely scenario—or scenarios—can be fully developed.

Where there is a real uncertainty about a development, the indicators of change from one probability to another can be identified. The result is then a "range" of most likely trends which becomes the *base case*.

It is against the base case that strategies can be developed that are robust or strong enough to reduce the element of surprise to a realistic and practical minimum. In addition, identifying and assessing the most likely range of trends and developments will provide an opportunity to consider designing and implementing strategies that can influence the proba-

Table 1. GLOBAL ECONOMY IN THE YEAR 2000
Key Assumptions/Facts

Characteristics/ Driving Forces	1950s	Entering the 1990s
• Global economic structure	• Independent nations • Superpower economic colonialism	• Global interdependence
• U.S. economic/policy view	• Global-positive sum game	• National-zero sum game
• Security	• Cold war • Nuclear build-up	• Thaw • Proliferation • Terrorism
• U.S. role	• Dominant • World police	• First among equals • Shared responsibility
• Global leadership	• Superpowers	• Void
• National policy focus	• Nationalism	• Nationalism/regionalism (despite global rhetoric)
• Ideology	• Reconstruction • Anticommunism	• Selfish • Liberalization
• World growth	• High	• Moderate
• World trade	• Accelerating	• Relative decline • Intraregional trade high
• Monetary flows	• U.S. DFI	• Globalization of DFI (U.S.–Europe–Asia triad)

Characteristics/ Driving Forces	1950s	Entering the 1990s
• Currencies	• Fixed and stable	• Floating and volatile
	• U.S.$ dominant	• Yen/DM/SFr dominance
		• U.S.$ vulnerable
• Technology	• U.S. clear lead	• Globalization/shared lead
	• Rest dependent on U.S. transfer	• Widespread access (but protected)
• Communications	• National	• Global
• Energy	• Cheap, "infinite"	• Expensive, finite, valued
	• Stable, controlled supply	• Volatile, independent supply
• U.S. competitiveness	• U.S. #1	• Stabilizing after 20 years of relative decline
• Europe economy	• Postwar reconstruction	• Regional rebirth
	• Birth of common market	• EC growing up
• Japan economy	• Postwar reconstruction	• Global dominance without global leadership
	• Start industrialization	• Towards postindustrial
• Developing countries	• Postcolonial birth	• NIEs—emerging global competitors
		• LDCs—debt crisis
• Environment	• Local	• Global
	• Low concern	• Serious problem
	• Focus on economic development	• Focus on sustainable development

bility of certain developments, thereby reducing constraints or indeed opening up favorable opportunities.

What follows is one attempt to construct four alternative scenarios, or visions of the future, of the global economy. The scenarios are based on the same driving forces, but with the outcomes reflecting differences in their evolution. The probability of each is assessed against current trends and information, and a base case, or most likely outcome, is described.

There are certain developments that will occur independently of all but the most extreme scenarios.

- *Population.* Population growth in the industrialized countries will remain very low and in some countries be negative. In the NICs (newly industrializing countries) population control plans will only be partially successful in restraining growth, and in the less developed countries, famine, war, and natural disasters will be the only constraints. The population is aging the world over due to improving health and living conditions.
- *The "Triad."* Though there will be variations in comparative status and influence, the world in the year 2000 will be dominated by Japan and its neighbors, North America, and Europe.
- *The U.S.* will remain a vanguard economy global power. At the same time the Japanese influence will have grown considerably.
- *The pace of change* in technology is unlikely to slow. The key constraining factor will be the availability of skills and capital to be able to exploit the development positively.
- *Life styles* will continue to change and converge, though national and local differences will become more or less important factors depending on the scenario.
- *Third World debt* will remain a continuing problem. It is only the degree of seriousness that changes under each of the scenarios.
- *The industrialized countries* will remain democracies. Demographic change will reduce labor market entry, and labor

productivity will be a continuing priority. The move to the
service-based economy will continue, the speech of acceptance being scenario-dependent.
• *The newly industrialized countries' growth* will be above the world
average. Their political stability may well still be fragile.
Their continuing requirement will be for new markets.

At the same time there are, of course, major macropolitical
and economic driving forces at work, the paths of which will
significantly affect the overall environment.

• In the U.S., the ability of the administration to contain and
reduce the twin deficits is a major driver. This will determine
whether the U.S. enjoys rapid economic growth in the early
1990s, whether protectionism is rife, or indeed whether
there is sufficient restructuring to reestablish U.S. global
competitiveness.
• For Europe, the main question is whether the dream of 1992
will be realized to the full. Any significant economic recession will result in a highly protectionist "fortress Europe,"
with serious consequences for world trade.
• In Japan, the years to 1992 will see whether Japan can
become a true international player economically and politically. If not, the likely alternative is a period of fierce, possibly militant, nationalism.
• Eastern Europe's future is critically dependent on the success of *perestroika*. If it fails, not only will the region revert to
economic despondency, trade with the rest of Europe will be
ruined, and the cold war could again resume.
• Latin America and Africa are faced with increasingly severe
debt crises. Economic—and political—breakdown has a
high probability. Low world prices for these countries' main
exports of commodities exacerbate the problem. Can and
indeed will the international community respond positively
and avert what is certain to be a major world financial crisis?
• Asia too is subject to uncertainty. Will the People's Republic
of China (PRC) be successful in liberalizing its economy—or
will it revert to its more traditional isolationism? South

Korea, Taiwan, Hong Kong, and Singapore are undergoing political and economic transformations. Unknowns include Singapore's future after Lee Kwan Yew, Hong Kong's integration with mainland China, Taiwan's and Korea's ability to combine political stability with accelerating liberalization.

• Other major uncertainties include governments' ability to contain inflation and indeed to reduce the volatility of exchange rates.

Year 2000 Scenario I:
Toward a Global Economy

The international financial system has achieved fragile stability. World GDP growth has averaged 3.5 percent to 4.5 percent over the past two to three years. Intercontinental trade has reflected a similar growth pattern and is fluctuating between 5.5 percent and 6.5 percent a year; trade in manufactures is stable at between 7 percent and 8 percent, and there has been a marked improvement in trade in services, now reaching 4 percent on a world basis and as high as 6.5 percent in the Organization for Economic Cooperation and Development (OECD) countries. Oil prices are stable but remain comparatively high at $20 per barrel (1989 U.S. dollars).

Capital flows are good and encouraging development in Latin America, especially Brazil. The U.S., having overcome the problems of the twin deficits by the mid-1990s, is showing every indication of a more balanced growth. The European Single Market, with Austria and Norway as new members and Switzerland and Sweden enjoying a special trade relationship, is experiencing a period of high growth at 4.5 percent; there is renewed talk of closer political federation. Japan has become a high value postindustrial economy, with only marginally slower growth rates than in the early years of the decade. It is very much a global vanguard economy.

This period of economic health, with the virtual disappearance of trade wars—there are only the spasmodic skirmishes—has been helped by a new stability in currencies. The yen, the

U.S. dollar, and the European ECU are strong and show only minor variations in exchange rates.

Communications and information access continue the breakdown of national borders begun in the late 1980s. Global radio and television broadcasting via satellites becomes commonplace, fulfilling Marshall McLuhan's vision of the "global village." As modern culture becomes more homogeneous, local differences matter less. Products are standardized, manufactured globally, and advertised and marketed. The regional trading blocs, having begun to form in the late 1980s and 1990s to help members build up competitive advantage, start to give way to interregional alliances.

Political regionalism begins to dissolve in response to extraordinary external forces: a debt crisis, an environmental disaster. International organizations such as the International Monetary Fund (IMF) and the United Nations Environment Program (UNEP) gain in power and become de facto "governments," in many cases superseding national authority. The greater similarity in world culture and the strength of the international authorities act as spurs to arms reductions, leading eventually to multilateral disarmament.

Current Probability: Low. Only a catastrophe of major proportions could cause nations to work against their nature and give up the power of self-determination. The only alternative—sustained superb global leadership—is highly unlikely. Nationalism and regionalism are stronger forces than global interdependence because they are more consistent with human nature, which tends more toward selfishness than altruism.

Year 2000 Scenario II:
Competitive Accommodation

International debt crises still occur, but the world financial system is able to cope. There have been effective compromises on debt reschedulings and capital is now flowing into the Latin American debtor nations. Africa still presents severe problems. World inflation rates have exhibited a slight downward trend for the past three years after peaking at dangerously high levels in the mid-1990s. The U.S. is faced with deficits, but the administration has managed to reduce them to a manageable amount; the country is by no means the world's biggest debtor nation.

World trade growth has been at 5 percent for the past two years, though intraregional trade shows somewhat higher growth rates. Nonetheless, protectionist pressures have generally reduced. Both the U.S. administration and European Commission have successfully vetoed protectionist legislation. GATT has made significant advances on agriculture and on trade in services, though on the latter, Third World countries continue to fight OECD moves. Oil prices have remained within a 10 percent price band over the past two years.

The European Community (EC) is now an effective global competitor in information technology and telecommunications, due to the success of strategic alliances engineered by leading globalized multinational corporations. Despite this, the Community is only just completing the last steps to turn the dream of 1992 into a solid reality. Recent economic summits have proved more effective than in the past. Exchange rates are stable though the U.S. dollar continues to show signs of uncertainty faced with the continuing strength of the yen.

The trend toward global cooperation is tempered by the need of the developing world to become globally competitive. Regional blocs, such as Europe post-1992 and North America (U.S./Canada/Mexico), view their role as allowing members to work out their competitive strategies in a controlled setting. With growing internationalization, the blocs also form interregional alliances: Europe with Japan, North America with developing Asia. International organizations work primarily on global quality-of-life issues such as the environment; because of cooperation from member states, they are reasonably successful at finding solutions.

There is an overall decline in emphasis on defense matters because of a generally high level of trust and the widespread perception that resources are better allocated toward improving competitiveness.

Current Probability: Moderate. The pragmatic need to stimulate growth and development could create "strange bedfellows." Nations may be willing to give up some sovereignty in exchange for competitive advantage in the global marketplace. Environmental and Third World welfare issues are already taking a higher profile, producing the need for nonpartisan leadership. The nature and quality of such leadership and its sustainability over a decade are, again, key questions.

Year 2000 Scenario III: Regional Self-Interest

World GNP growth rates have been disappointing, averaging 2.5 percent to 3 percent a year since the mid-1990s. Growth on a regional basis has, however, been stronger. Intraregional trade grew by as much as 5 percent in the last two years of the decade. The main increase has been in manufactures, with trade in services being slow to catch up. Indeed, the GATT Accord on Services has not been reached, with the European Community remaining at odds with the U.S. and Japan.

Oil prices remain weak and fluctuating; since 1998, they have ranged between $17.50 and $21 per barrel (1989 U.S. dollars). Capital flows have been sluggish, with the industrialized countries having shown a marked reluctance to invest in Latin America and other major debtor nations, the one exception—and that is a sporadic one—being Japan. The situation is now beginning to improve.

The world financial system is still subject to periodic crises—though these are decreasing—and the decade has seen a series of major moratoriums. The U.S., still faced with major deficits, has been focusing increasingly on the North American market. Europe continues to show marked protectionist tendencies; in many ways, fortress Europe has become a reality to many Asian and U.S. companies. Japan dominates Asia; the relationships with the PRC, Taiwan, and Korea are strained, though the dependence of the latter group on Japan is reluctantly recognized. The PRC is once again experiencing overheating, not helped by the inability to integrate Hong Kong into the mainland economy; politically there has been a swing back to increased state power.

The Eastern bloc has failed to achieve the growth rates outlined as part of the goals of *perestroika* in the early years of the 1990s. The Western powers' economic summits have only proved marginally effective. After a decade of volatility, interest rates are at long last becoming more stable, as are exchange rates. Governments continue to implement economic programs characterized by short termism, with scant regard for longer-term impacts.

Economic issues predominate as competition intensifies the trend toward regionalism. Trading blocs take on a more political character; protectionism increases, as does the likelihood of trade wars. Regional defense organizations such as NATO find renewed purpose even in an environment of reduced nuclear weapons. Distrust persists between blocs; superpower relations, while not worsening, do not improve much. International leadership fails to stimulate cooperation even on critical issues; leading nations attempt unilateral solutions to problems such as Third World debt, with only mixed results.

Current Probability: High. Europe 1992 and the U.S.–Canada Free Trade Agreement have already produced global trade frictions, leading to the presumption of "fortress Europe" and a North American bloc. Global leadership on protectionism and debt issues appears to be dormant.

Year 2000 Scenario IV:
National Self-Interest

The international financial system hovers on the edge of collapse. World GDP growth has been at best minimal at 1.5

percent to 2.5 percent a year; though Japan and East Asia continue to perform well ahead of the world average. Intraregional trade has not realized the promise of the early years of the decade, and intercontinental trade has been static. GATT accords are regularly breached and GATT has failed to reach agreement in trade in services. There are trade wars on agriculture, textiles, and many manufactured goods between the U.S., Japan, and Europe. Oil prices are now at an all-time high.

There are no or very little international capital flows; as a result the economies of the major debtor nations (Latin America) remain in a highly perilous state. Currencies fluctuate wildly, though the yen has maintained its strength vis-à-vis the U.S. dollar and the German DM fairly consistently over the past three years.

Not surprisingly, governments continue to introduce ever more restricting protectionist legislation. The economies of Eastern Europe are still suffering the shocks of the failure of *perestroika*. The PRC is retreating into a new period of isolationism, despite moves by Japan and the recovery of Hong Kong.

The maneuvering en route to the creation of regional groupings has degenerated into full-scale global trade war. "Europe 1992" has been exposed as a scheme to benefit the strong countries and exploit the weak; the strong (France, Germany, and the U.K.) disagree over sovereignty and reciprocity issues and decide to take their chances on their own. Meanwhile, Japan's yen-driven economic aggressiveness provokes trade sanctions by the U.S. Military distrust increases, prompting calls for a halt to disarmament and even a new arms build-up.

Developed countries find monetary reserves sapped by the pressures of military build-up, maintaining social services, and virtually solo global competition; social services are the loser. Developing countries are subjected to stringent conditions by their creditors. International organizations are effectively powerless.

Current Probability: Low. To move toward what would effectively be global isolationism would be to negate two decades of technological advances and political alliances. As "peace breaks out all over" in 1989, and nations recognize the need for global cooperation on some levels, it seems unlikely that a deterioration could be caused except by extremely unwise unilateral action by one of the global economic powers.

"Base Case": The Most Likely Outcome

The world is at a crossroads, faced both politically and economically with volatility and uncertainty. The most likely range of outcomes is bounded by two paths which carry very different consequences.

In the short term the most likely path to the two boundaries is the same, with the world muddling through and leaving the critical issues unresolved. Then along one boundary there could be real moves to stabilize the world economic situation, and by 1995, governments, realizing their pragmatic requirements to work together, will have reached the state of "competitive accommodation," particularly to maintain a relatively free, albeit managed, world trading system, to manage the debt crisis, and to reduce volatility in interest rates and currencies. The course of events to 2000 remains reasonably smooth (Scenario II).

The alternative path, which forms the other boundary in the base case range, shows a world to 2000 of declining global economic cooperation and sustained high volatility. On this path, by 1993–1994, increased protectionism and intraregional developments will have led to a world well on the way to being organized in regional blocs (Europe, Asia, North America). By the end of the decade, each of the blocs will have erected protectionist barriers acting as a constraint on real growth (Scenario III).

The two worlds of "competitive accommodation" and "regional self-interest" are very different. *Most current indicators point to a much higher likelihood of the regional self-interest scenario.*

This assessment derives from what seem now to be the most likely outcomes in the following:

- *The U.S.:* response to the twin deficits is likely to be too little and too late, fueling uncertainty and squabbles between major governments and increasing protectionism.
- *Europe,* while making progress to its goals, will be somewhat frustrated by its inability to move fast enough to regain competitiveness. Protectionism will increase in retaliation to the U.S. and in defense against Japan and Korea.
- *Japan's* moves to internationalization are likely to have only limited success, leading to some nationalistic backlash. Some, by no means all, Japanese companies will continue to invest in Europe and the U.S. as a defense against protectionism.
- *The USSR* faces enormous difficulties but continued, albeit very slow and painful, progress to liberalization is likely to continue, because there are no alternatives other than total stagnation.
- *The PRC* is likely to move much more slowly than the hopes of the optimists; the chances of a serious reversal of policies are reducing marginally.
- *The debt crisis* will not be satisfactorily resolved, although the international financial community is likely to move just far enough to avoid a total breakdown in the system.
- *The East Asian countries* seem likely to go through their transformation, with considerable political and social turbulence, but without significant disruption to their economic development. Hong Kong will become increasingly tied to the PRC.
- *The strongest economies* (U.S., Japan, Germany) will increase their dominance, particularly within their regional blocs.
- *A more isolationist U.S.* will stress self-sufficiency, often at the expense of international cooperation.
- *The NICs* will show some decline in their growth rates.
- *The high-debt countries* in Latin America, such as Brazil and Mexico, will suffer further serious deterioration.

Characteristics of the Global
Economy in the Year 2000

1. Economic Indicators for Base Case Scenario—
Toward Regional Self-Interest

Table 2.

(a) Economic forecast			
	Current (89/90)	1995	2000
World GDP (%)	2.5	2.5–3.0	3.0
• N. America	2.0–2.5	2.5–3.0	3.0
• Europe	2.0–2.5	2.5–3.0	3.0
• Asia	2.5–3.5	4.0–5.0	5.0
• Latin America	2.5–3.5	4.0–5.0	5.0+
OECD inflation	4.0–4.5	4.5–5.5	4.0–5.0
Trade growth			
• intercontinental	2.5–3.5	3.0–4.0	2.5–3.5
• intraregional	4.0–5.0	5.0–6.0	5.5
• manufactures	6.0–7.0	7.0–8.0	6.0–7.0
Oil price (per barrel)	$13.50–15	$15–20	$17.50–21
	depressed	volatile	firming
Interest rates (U.S. prime;	rising	falling	stable
others track)	11.0–11.5	9.5–10.5	9.0

2. Global Competitiveness

Increasing regionalism has focused economic growth and competition in and on the triad. To varying degrees, each of the major blocs has become protectionist and isolationist, fortress Europe being at one extreme and Japan at the other. As a result, Japan is increasing its investments in Latin America and Southeast Asia. Overall, competition is now a defensive tactic relying—to an extent—on nontariff trade barriers. There is a lack of open dynamism, the only saving grace being the at-

(b) Economic Trends	Current (89/90)	1995	2000
Debt	volatile; default (?)	rescheduling and renegotiation	declining but remains problem
• capital flows	constrained	moderate growth	picking up, renewed flows
Exchange rates	volatile: $ weakens Y strengthens	less volatility; $, Y strengthen	stabilizing; block systems
U.S.	Minimal adjustment in deficits. Int'l confidence volatile. Slowing economy.	Large but declining deficits. More insular. North American focus.	Fast reduction in deficits. Lower trade dependence.
Japan	Strong growth (tail winds). Large trade imbalances.	Specializing, high value economy. Focus on Asia. Moves to internationalize.	Dominates Asia. Breaks free of cycles.
Europe	Moderate growth. Continued move toward 1992. Importance of intra-European trade increases.	Towards 1992. Continued moderate growth.	Realization of 1992. Fortress Europe (?)

tempts of a few leading high-tech multinationals to redress the balance.

Korea is a full member of the OECD, and Taiwan enjoys—like Yugoslavia—a special relationship. At the same time, the trend to regionalism has meant that ASEAN has become a more coordinated economic bloc, though not yet a common market. Brazil and Argentina are cooperating more closely and developing further trading links with southern Africa, India, and the Eastern bloc.

The European Community is currently negotiating membership terms with Austria and Norway, and hoping to finalize the "special relationships" with Switzerland and Sweden, which will ensure—in the short term at any rate—a high degree of European self-sufficiency. Trade with the Eastern bloc countries is consolidating, but still reliant on barter to an excessive extent. The invigoration of the Soviet economy and those of its allies has not been nearly so successful as was hoped; nonetheless there have been significant improvements, and a few Western multinational companies owe their current prosperity to early moves into Eastern Europe.

Table 3.

THE TREND SETTERS
   Global economic and political powers, and leaders of the regional blocs
   • *United States*, leading Canada and Mexico
   • *Europe*, led by Germany, France and the U.K.
   • *Japan*, leading Korea and the Asian NIEs (Singapore, Indonesia,
     Malaysia, Thailand).

THE CATCH-UPS OR HAS-BEENS
   Countries/regions with potential to play significant global economic
   roles but enormous political, economic, or social obstacles to overcome
   • *USSR*
   • *Eastern bloc countries*
   • *Taiwan*
   • *Brazil*
   • *People's Republic of China*
   • *India*

THE POTENTIAL SPOILERS
   Strategically important trouble spots, highly volatile
   • *Middle East*
   • *Southern Africa*
   • *Latin America (excluding Brazil)*

THE "ORPHANS AT THE FEAST"
   Countries or regions with problems so deep-seated as to prevent
   development even with global intervention
   • *Africa*
   • *remainder of Third World*

---

3. Currencies

Exchange rates are stabilizing. Three regional currency blocs coexist moderately well. The European Currency Unit is a fully negotiable currency and this fact has helped stabilize the European Monetary System.

The U.S. dollar remains, of course, a major currency and does not fluctuate as much as it did in the early 1990s against the Deutsche mark and the yen. The yen itself is now the negotiating currency for East and Southeast Asia. Austria and New Zealand traders are quoting more often in yen than in U.S. dollars! One of the stabilizing elements is undoubtedly the economic summits.

4. The Role of the Multinational Company

The multinational company (MNC) is more than ever a global economic force, and shows every sign of becoming a strong political influence as well. Its role varies depending upon the home country and upon its product line.

In the OECD countries there is much closer cooperation between MNCs and the nation-state than at any time in the past—indeed, the trend toward corporate statism is pronounced. In Europe, this is showing itself at Community level. At the same time, MNCs are the one driving force toward increased globalization and away from the prevalent regionalism and nationalism. However, doubts are emerging about the legitimacy of the multinational company's role—and pressure is mounting in such organizations as the OECD to regulate MNC power.

5. International Debt

The level of international debt has declined somewhat. Nonetheless the problem remains serious. Key areas of concern are Africa, where the cycle of depression appears permanent, some countries in Eastern Europe (e.g., Bulgaria and Rumania), Peru, and the smaller Latin American countries. Brazil, Argentina, and Mexico have been able to avoid major reschedulings. Capital outflow has ceased and investment is increasing in key economic sectors. Nonetheless the improvements are both slight and fragile. Inflation remains a problem but the creditor nations are negotiating from a longer-term perspective than in the past.

6. Global Investment Flows

Investment flows continue to be influenced by the behavior of international debt. The liberalization of capital markets and the twenty-four-hour a day seven-day a week operation of these markets led to a volatility in world markets which is only now settling down. The future looks promising—but an element of high uncertainty remains.

7. International Intergovernmental Organizations

The shifts in economic power gave Japan a much greater role in the World Bank and the IMF. Korea is now urging increased participation in decision making in such organizations for itself. Nonetheless, the U.S. and Europe still act as major influences, though to a reduced extent.

The World Bank and its associate, the IMF, are cooperating more closely with other UN agencies in underscoring the need for sustainable development in the Third World. With the reduction in political rhetoric in the UN, the technical agencies are proving more successful in ensuring material progress in many countries. UN agencies now actively seek the cooperation of the private sector in implementing projects—and have some success.

The debate at GATT continues over trade in services, the Third World countries maintaining that they are being constrained in their development by the proposals of the U.S. and—to a lesser extent—Europe. There are still avoidable clashes over trade in agriculture.

There is greater international cooperation on noneconomic issues such as environmental protection and controlling the spread of such diseases as AIDS.

8. Labor

Demographic change and the further application of technology have altered the profile of the work force. In the industrialized countries, fewer critical skills shortages are appearing than in the past. Productivity remains a key issue, particularly in the U.S. and Western Europe but less so in Japan. Work organization is now more flexible than at any time in the past, with semiautonomous work units, flextime, and teleworking increasingly common.

In the NICs, due in part to the failure of the West to totally satisfactorily transfer technology, there are critical skill shortages. This is now being corrected. Unemployment is reducing with the slow decrease in labor force entry. In Latin America and the less developed countries, underemployment and unemployment are major problems; the only reason they are not endangering social stability is the size of the parallel economy.

- *Use of military force.* Superpower intervention will become less common as the U.S. and USSR develop closer understanding and concentrate on domestic issues. Any conflict will probably stem from ideological or religious causes and will be geographically contained. The exception will be a U.S. or NATO response to terrorism.

Role of the United States in the Year 2000: Some Implications

The U.S. As Superpower

Even in an era of greater cooperation and fewer overt conflicts, there will remain a need for a military balance of power.

A more cooperative, less interventionist United States would be able to counterbalance the USSR politically and Japan and Europe economically (probably as leader of a North American alliance).

In global affairs, America will continue to be in the vanguard, albeit only as one of several power centers. The U.S. will potentially continue to have a major role as the catalyst for international cooperation on global issues; to do this it will need to capitalize on its traditional position as the leader of the free world by continuing to be a vocal and active proponent of basic freedoms, human rights, and free trade.

The U.S. as a whole is likely to find itself isolated economically, partly as a result of its own increasingly protectionist isolationist policies. However, many individual U.S. companies will position themselves to succeed in the global arena.

Relations with Asia

Despite many predictions, there is an increasing number of experts who maintain that the year 2000 will not, in fact, be the beginning of the "Pacific Century": the Asian countries are too heterogeneous to unite as a political force, and economic growth is expected to slow significantly from the giddy heights of the 1980s and early 1990s. In addition, cultural similarities with Europe cause many to believe that the U.S. will continue to look across the Atlantic well into the next century.

American interests will undoubtedly increase in Asia for a variety of reasons. Japan's ascendance as an economic power, and its evident desire to increase trading links with the Soviet Union, will produce an uneasy relationship with the U.S. At the same time, the other Asian nations, most notably Korea and Taiwan, look to the U.S. to provide a balance to the power of Japan. A stronger Association of Southeast Asian Nations (ASEAN) or other multinational organization or multinational company will be the conduit for the U.S.'s involvement in the region.

Relations with Europe

The perception of the Single European Act as an attempt to create "fortress Europe" will be a self-fulfilling prophecy to the extent that the U.S. maintains its protectionist posture. The U.S. will still be seen as a military protector, but with strictly limited ability to enforce its will militarily. The EC will increasingly want to stress its independence both economically and strategically. It will try to exert a defense role, thereby weakening NATO.

The U.S. will need to work with a unified Europe as a partner and ally on middle-of-the-road global issues such as environmental protection. In fact, with the EC member states potentially spanning the ideological spectrum from Thatcherite to Euro-Communist, dealings with the Community as a whole will have to remain apolitical.

Relations with the Third World

Debt restructuring, sustainable development, and political stability will all require international intervention. The U.S. needs to and will play a key role, at times a leading role. In contrast to the past, however, its power to dictate terms will be severely limited by reduced military credibility and burdens on available funds. Greater effort will be made at persuasion, perhaps by tying economic aid to initiatives in social areas; the U.S. will stumble a few times in its attempts to be a gentler, kinder persuader.

Final Report of the Seventy-Sixth American Assembly

A t the close of their discussions the participants in the Seventy-sixth American Assembly, on *U.S. Interests in the 1990s: Managing the Global Economy,* at Arden House, Harriman, New York, April 20–23, 1989, reviewed as a group the following statement. This statement represents general agreement; however, no one was asked to sign it. Furthermore, it should be understood that not everyone agreed with all of it.

Preamble

Dramatic changes have taken place in the global economy—and the pace is likely to continue at a relentless rate. We see the next few years as a watershed—a significant turning point in post-World War II political, economic, and security relations. It is a uniquely promising moment in history, when Western Europe is moving toward unity; Japan has attained great economic power and is seeking appropriate world responsibilities; the Soviet Union, several nations in Eastern Europe, and China are turning away from doctrinaire communism to attempt economic and political reforms; and many developing countries have emerged as pace-setters in political and economic reform. In short, we have relative peace and many shared political and economic goals—a large number of which have been inspired by U.S. example. Moreover, this remarkable moment in history is formed by a fast-moving, multidimensional technological revolution that has heightened the increasing interdependence of nations.

Yet, at a time that should be triumphant, the industrialized democracies have permitted dangerous trade and other economic imbalances to build up within the international system. Unless corrected soon, they could engulf the world in a new wave of protectionism and bring a financial crisis in the 1990s. Those imbalances are rooted in mistaken and often self-indulgent domestic policies of the industrialized democracies. Responsibility for ensuring a healthy international economy now rests primarily upon domestic policy changes in the United States, Japan, and Western Europe. It is urgent that the leaders of those nations act quickly and decisively. The 1990s represent a decade of enormous opportunity, but we must no longer ignore the growing dangers.

We need to seize the moment to create a new architecture for international economic cooperation, one that takes advantage of the economic strength many of our friends and allies have attained in recent years. We need to promote global growth, expand and liberalize trade, strengthen the international development effort, and address issues such as drugs and environmental deterioration, which affect virtually all nations acutely.

Constructing this new architecture poses an exciting challenge to American leadership. Having risen to the task of rebuilding the global economy after World War II, the United States is at a point in history when it must again exert leadership, as it did then, to develop a comprehensive strategy for addressing the myriad issues before the international economy. This time the United States can act with the help of a group of nations that were unable to play a major role in the 1940s, but they can and must now share responsibility for providing the ideas, leadership, and resources necessary to meet the challenges ahead.

The world has made remarkable economic progress since the devastation of World War II—and Americans should feel a strong sense of pride that their nation's leadership has played a critical role in this success. Most of the goals set by the United States for achieving a stronger and more prosperous democratic world over the last forty years have been met beyond expectations: Western Europe and Japan are thriving and prosperous democracies, market economics has demonstrated its superiority to communism, and world trade and investment have expanded dramatically.

What then should our goals be, what policy instruments should be employed to achieve them, and what institutional structures are best suited to the tasks ahead?

The economic and political relationships among nations and the underlying characteristics of the global economy today differ greatly from those of the 1940s, when current international institutions were created. And by the end of this century they will be far different still. Today the freedom of capital flow exerts powerful constraints on national management; burgeoning populations in the developing world exert massive pressures for migration; governments increasingly seek to manage flows of trade and direct investment; the forces of economic nationalism have become stronger as globalization of the world economy renders workers and industries more vulnerable to international forces; nations artificially create competitive advantage to the detriment of others; trade and current account imbalances reflect large domestic imbalances in the United States and its trading partners; populations have come to realize how vulnerable they are to one another's lack of environmental responsibility; remarkable changes in the previously rigid economies in the Communist world reflect recognition that they lack global competitiveness and are unable to meet the basic needs of their citizens; the world's poorer nations, most of them debt-encumbered, are experiencing enormous human and economic problems which portend social volatility and international instability; and technological changes cause quick shifts in competitive advantage and bring the world closer together by permitting the instant and massive dissemination of information and ideas.

Leaders and officials under pressure of time and politics must make choices that will influence the course of our lives and societies. Often what appear to be insurmountable political or resource constraints to new policies or shifts in priorities, attitudes, or patterns of resource allocation can be overcome if benefits of doing so, or the costly implications of not doing so, are made dramatically clear. President Franklin Roosevelt conveyed a sense of the costs to America of failing to provide Britain with lend-lease aid by explaining the importance of helping a neighbor to put out the fire in his home lest it next spread to yours.

It is frequently asserted that democracies take bold decisions only in crisis. In the current environment it is essential to build a new architecture of international economic cooperation and address internal economic problems, to avert a crisis. Failure to act puts the United States in harm's way—vulnerable to an energy crisis as our import dependence increases, vulnerable to a financial crisis as domestic and international deficits and our attendant dependence on massive imports of foreign capital persist, vulnerable to an outbreak of economic nationalism as trade issues and imbalances go unattended to, vulnerable to massive instability in the Third World along with massive immigration pressures as the debt problem festers, vulnerable to unexampled dangers to the physical environment, and vulnerable to the geopolitical consequences of instability in Eastern Europe as their economies deteriorate. Even if such crises never occur, insufficiently bold action on the domestic and international economic fronts will mean a steady drift that renders us less and less capable of influencing events and saps American leadership potential and spirit.

First Among Equals: Relations with Japan and Europe

From being first, the United States has become first among equals, its main rivals also being its closest allies: the European Community (EC) and Japan. The difficulties thus created stem in large measure from the success of earlier American initiatives. Economic reconstruction of Western Europe and Japan and the political integration of the European Community were, with the successful containment of the USSR, the principal strategic goals of the United States in the postwar world.

Goal of Cooperative Global Economic Management

With the exception of the much more urgent concern about the global environment, the goals of the United States in managing the global economy are essentially what they have always been: sustained economic growth on the basis of an open, market oriented global economy. What has changed is the ability of the United States to achieve this goal on its own. While the United States can and should remain the leader for the foreseeable future, to do so it will have to improve its own economic performance by managing its own affairs more successfully and cooperating more effectively with Japan and the European Community than it has succeeded in doing up to now. There will be frictions, but these are containable—and must be contained.

A prime U.S. policy goal in dealing with Japan and the European Community must be genuine partnership, beginning with economic and financial responsibility sharing. For political as much as economic reasons, the American people increasingly believe they are paying too high a cost and a disproportionate share of the costs for leadership in security, world economic development, and maintenance of the world trading system.

The existing international institutions, both formal—the International Monetary Fund (IMF), the World Bank, the regional development banks, the General Agreement on Tariffs and Trade (GATT), the Organization for Economic Cooperation and Development (OECD), and the relevant U.N. agencies—and informal—the Groups of Five and Seven—need to be reinforced. This is particularly true of the problem of the global environment, where the increasing cogency of the issue demands a more effective institutional framework. There will also have to be reallocation of responsibilities, with Japan, for example, being encouraged to play a far bigger and more positive role.

Successful global policy coordination requires not merely the constant cooperation of the United States, Japan, and West Germany within the evolving EC institutional framework, but willingness of all the main newly industrializing countries (NICs), including the primary NICs such as Korea and Taiwan, to align the pursuit of domestic and international goals. Without such coordination, governments cannot expect to achieve and maintain the growth of the world economy, price stability, and exchange rate stability. The ongoing effort to achieve more stable exchange rates can in turn help to focus attention on the need for mutually compatible changes in domestic policies.

In trade, too, the multilateral system embodied in the GATT must remain the cornerstone of U.S. policy and must be strengthened through successful completion of the Uruguay Round. But this will not be enough to preserve it. The United States is also committed to market-opening strategies of a unilateral and bilateral character aimed at achieving more equitable access to markets. The United States must be mindful of the need to pursue these strategies in ways that complement and reinforce the multilateral objective and promote the fundamental goal of a more liberal world economy.

The Emergence of a New Power—Europe 1992

A new kind of entity is emerging in Western Europe, one characterized by ever greater pooling of sovereignty in economic affairs. For a long time, the United States will have to deal simultaneously with both the EC institutions and the member states, especially the major ones. But relations with the community institutions, and in particular the Commission, should be upgraded.

The European Community's program for completing the internal market should be regarded as an opportunity rather than as a threat. For the Europeans themselves it represents a further step toward an essentially political vision. For the United States it should be no more controversial than all the previous stages toward its longstanding goal of strengthening Western Europe. To date, the risk of a "fortress Europe" has been greatly exaggerated, and what risks of increased protection there are can be averted by purposeful U.S. and multilateral action, to which the European Community generally has shown itself sensitive.

Despite the absence of any broad protectionist objective, there are risks in emerging EC trade policy—in antidumping, in local content requirements, in reciprocity, and in the replacement of national quota restriction by EC-wide measures. The United States can—and must—tackle these, largely through the Uruguay Round, but also in bilateral forums.

On the other portion of the European continent, the collapse of the Communist model represents one of the great changes in the world and a positive development for the United States and its allies. But smug self-satisfaction is not the right response. Efforts need to be made, consistent with maintenance of Western security, to bring Eastern European countries into the world economy. The European Community is clearly in the best position to achieve this. It should be encouraged to do so.

A Crucial Bilateral Relationship—Japan

Japan, the world's first economic superpower without military power, is embarking on a historic, domestic debate about the nature of its global responsibilities and long-range interests. The United States also stands at a historic juncture regarding its global responsibilities. These two democracies must fundamentally reassess the nature of their partnership.

Yet the U.S.–Japan relationship suffers from intense conflicts over important economic interests. The United States is growing increasingly frustrated by the limited results of endless attempts to penetrate the Japanese markets, whether in semiconductors, supercomputers, agriculture, or consumer goods. On the other hand, the Japanese rightly argue that the United States lacks a responsible fiscal policy and adequate savings rate. There are real risks from this state of mutual recrimination.

Immediate disputes must be resolved—and a wider cooperative vision put in its place. Japan must import substantially more manufactured goods. The current account surplus is both a political and an economic problem. It has fallen from 4.4 percent of Japan's GNP in 1986 to 2.9 percent last year. It should fall further and more of the surplus should go to the developing countries.

Japan must be encouraged to proceed faster toward implementing the vision of its role in the world economy indicated in the Maekawa report, one in which growth is driven largely by domestic demand at home and greater governmental attention is given to constructive engagement abroad, especially in the developing world. There is also a need to find opportunities for additional shared activities. The immense challenges of addressing the global environmental changes and Third World debt present an important opportunity in that regard.

A Vastly Different Third World

A stable, growing world economy that meets U.S. interests must include the active participation of the Third World. The failure to deal with a vastly changed, but often ignored, Third World is potentially explosive. In the decade ahead, developing countries must be part of the solution to many problems confronting the industrialized world—from the U.S. trade deficit to the scourge of narcotics.

The Third World covers a broad spectrum of nations that includes such new industrial powerhouses as South Korea, such nations as Mexico where economic potential is hobbled by debt, and the desperately poor lands of sub-Saharan Africa, where living standards have sharply eroded in recent years.

Difficulties of Developing Countries

If debt burdens are not eased soon, some Latin American countries are likely to erupt with social and political turbulence. Rather than waiting for a crisis, prompt action can prevent one. Renewing growth and investment in developing countries will restore a valuable market for U.S. exports. Thus, helping the Third World reduce its debt burden is not only charity, but also enlightened self-interest.

Sustaining the global environment provides a major new challenge in relations with developing countries. The apparent warming of the world climate is likely to widen the gap between the developed and developing world. Dealing with this issue will require urgent policy choices and new forms of cooperation by all nations. The implications of failing to act range from rising sea levels through the renewed threat of famine due to possible failures in agricultural production. Dealing with this issue will require urgent policy changes by all nations. Industrialized countries must reduce their use of energy; new energy strategies, based on highly efficient technologies, must be developed and transferred to the Third World; and developing countries must address the task of slowing and reversing deforestation.

Great advances in improving well-being have been achieved in the past three decades, but much remains to be done to alleviate poverty in the foreseeable future. Sub-Saharan Africa, where explosive population growth is combined with severe environmental degradation, requires priority attention.

The shared social problems of illegal narcotics and AIDS demonstrate that the Third World is not a remote concern, but part of our own lives. AIDS epidemics are apparently most serious in Africa, the Caribbean, Europe, and North America.

And the rising tide of illicit drugs entering developed countries is a significant and increasingly divisive factor in relations with the developing world. Clearly, these common plagues require cooperation.

Ultimately, the developing countries themselves must take the tough steps necessary to attain growth. They must overcome formidable internal constraints arising from inefficient state economic controls. Some Third World regimes use their development problems as an excuse for human rights violation and outright corruption, which themselves retard development progress. Steps must be taken to slow rapid population growth if the task of providing jobs and meeting basic human needs is to be within the realm of the possible.

Developing countries willing to help themselves also need international support and encouragement that the United States has failed to provide. What can the United States do given its budgetary and other constraints? Considerably more than it is doing. The United States needs a coherent, predictable, long-term program for a differentiated and much more important Third World. Sustained and rapid economic growth in this area, particularly the middle-income developing countries now heavily burdened with debt, can be a key element in reducing the U.S. trade deficit without inducing a global recession. Some of the elements in a differentiating package for the Third World should include: support for human development programs and for opening up of their economies in south Asia; long-term twenty-year commitment to accelerating African development through a major reallocation of concessional flows; specific plans for reduction of debt burdens in middle-income countries, particularly in Latin America.

A Global Compact

The coming of a new president to power coincides with an extraordinary opportunity to create a more open and peaceful international system. It is essential that the United States articulate a clear sense of the world it would like to see and how it would like to get there. Many other nations do not yet know what role the United States wants for itself, much less others. At the same time, these countries not only accept the idea of U.S. leadership, they see no alternative. Yet, the current push for managed trade in Washington suggests that many Americans want an aggressive internationalism with the United States pursuing more confrontational policies against new economic "enemies," above all Japan. Recurrent calls for burden-shifting and bringing home American troops suggest that others want a return to neo-isolationism.

It is the firm recommendation of this Assembly that President Bush and Congress reject those cramped visions and embrace another that is far more positive and hopeful: *shared leadership*. There must be a greater opening of foreign markets and a greater sharing of military burdens, but the United States should remain committed to the strategic vision that has been immensely successful since the war: continued world economic growth, economic stability, open trade and investment, and a more equal distribution of economic resources through higher growth rates in developing countries. To those traditional goals must now be added another rapidly growing in significance: a healthy environment.

Reaching a Global Compact

The industrialized democracies now face a clear and present danger that unless they soon take corrective actions at home, the imbalances could bring on a financial earthquake during the early 1990s. The first fissure already appeared during the stock market crash of 1987. Unfortunately, several of these nations have demonstrated an inability to overcome their own domestic constraints. The United States has talked incessantly about its chronic budget deficits, but those deficits are bigger today than two years ago. The agreement recently reached by the president and Congress is wholly inadequate to correct the problem. In like measure, Japan has promised to adopt a more globalized economy, but the results of its reforms—while welcome—are still inadequate.

This Assembly strongly and urgently recommends that the

United States now take the lead in reaching a compact with the other industrialized democracies that commits each of them to put in place domestic measures that are desperately needed. President Bush should seize the opportunity at the coming Seven Nation Economic Summit this July to begin negotiating this compact. The G-7 mechanism for surveillance and policy coordination should be employed to monitor progress in carrying out this accord, and the IMF should be given a more prominent and transparent role in this evolving mechanism. In addition, the president should work with Congress to appoint a private bipartisan group in the United States who can work with the federal government to monitor progress. A global compact, taken seriously, would not only ensure each nation that it would realize significant benefit for taking tough political steps at home but would also provide an additional—and much needed—source of discipline upon it.

To what should the nations agree? This Assembly recommends the following measures:

* The United States. The United States must reestablish its international credibility and begin to deal with its domestic problems.

For its own sake, and for the world economy, the United States must finally put its economic house in order.

For years the nation has borrowed more than it has saved, spent more than it has earned, and bought more than it has produced. The result: a huge and growing external debt, high real interest rates, and lower investment in its markets than its competitors.

A critical first step is to balance the federal budget. We agree with President Bush's desire to first eliminate unnecessary spending. Nor would we exempt any area, including defense or entitlements, from this careful scrutiny. While respecting his desire to avoid raising taxes, and especially tax rates, we note elsewhere in this report and in the president's message to Congress an urgent need for additional expenditures in certain critical areas such as education. We believe that the funding of these essential programs and the needs of the total economy for more growth, lower interest rates, and reduced inflation will require significantly higher revenues.

This Assembly recommends, as part of a package of fiscal measures, that gasoline taxes be significantly and gradually raised as a means of achieving balance, reducing the rate of consumption growth, and lessening the nation's dependence on foreign oil, the largest American import. It must be adjusted, we agree, to eliminate regional and personal inequities—but this can be done. Adoption of a gas tax would reveal to the American people and the world that the U.S. government still has a capacity to act. We also look favorably upon "sin" taxes, a value added tax, and user fees. The sum of the new revenues raised should equal $50 billion per year. In parallel with this, a new effort is required to raise consistently the level of private American savings—and new techniques must be explored for doing this.

Japan. Despite many changes, Japan has moved too slowly to open its borders, and resentments are building to dangerous levels. As its part of a global compact, Japan should fully and speedily carry out its own commitment to the Maekawa report, globalizing its economy. Japan should also pay special attention to a series of additional measures: reform of its distribution system; a rationalization of its land and rice policies; an increase of its official development assistance to at least 1 percent of its GNP (although the Japanese participants viewed this figure as unrealistic), all of it untied; recycling its surpluses to urgent needs in the Third World, in the form of ODA, debt relief or otherwise, on a far larger scale; a reduction in the anticonsumption bias in its tax policy; and enforcement of antimonopoly laws.

* *The European Community.* President Bush should specifically welcome the economic and political integration of Europe, recognizing that it is a positive development for the United States and a contribution to world economic growth.

The European Community should supplement the 1992 program with accompanying policies aimed at increasing growth. In addition, the European Community should pledge to reduce average trade barriers to the lowest level of any of its constituent members, so passing on some of the internal benefits of its growth to others. The European Community, like the United States and Japan, should also reduce substantially its subsidies and protection associated with its agricultural policy, as well as liberalize its nontariff barriers (NTBs) and play a more concerted and constructive role in the Uruguay Round. It should make transparent and eliminate gray area measures such as interindustry, trade-restricting arrangements. We would welcome further changes in the European Community that would allow it to speak with a single voice in international economic institutions.

These measures, taken together, should bring significant progress toward reducing the current imbalances in world trade and placing the international economy on a smoother path through the 1990s. Current imbalances are unsustainable. The United States has a keen self interest in substantially reducing its level of borrowing from overseas. It must not be forgotten that while trilateral understandings on global issues are extremely important, any viable solutions to global problems must fully recognize the interests and responsibilities of the Third World and should be implemented through multilateral institutions.

A Broader Agenda for the United States

Over the long haul, the capacity of the United States to play a decisive role in world leadership depends upon its political will to deal with current problems, thereby insuring its continuing economic strength. Such leadership will be substantially enhanced if U.S. real GNP grows long term at least as fast as most, and preferably all, major industrialized economies with similar per capita incomes. In addition to the measures enumerated above, this Assembly recommends that the nation adopt a sweeping series of additional changes to strengthen its competitiveness and improve its prospects during the 1990s:

* *Education.* While its institutions of higher education are among the finest in the world, the U.S. system of primary and secondary schools is sorely inadequate for its domestic and international needs. The nation must invest not only more money but more time on the part of parents and other adults in the education of the next generation. A radical effort to improve teacher and student performance in grades pre-school through 12 is an absolute imperative, as is the effective employment of the newest educational technologies, especially for continuing education.

* *Infrastructure.* The disrepair of many roads and bridges, growing inefficiencies in other forms of transportation, and inadequate water and sewage systems hobble the country's ability to compete. The nation must seek a national infrastructure strategy and be prepared to invest several hundred billion dollars over the next few decades.

* *Government Regulation.* Care should be taken that anti-trust, communication, tax, and other regulatory policies not inhibit the competitiveness of U.S. industries.

* *Technologies.* U.S. policies should enhance the competitiveness of its industries. Strong support should be given to lowering the cost of capital. In some cases, promotion of industry may be essential to the national interest and the United States should provide support, especially for basic and process research. A regulatory environment should be created that fosters procompetitive cooperative activities, particularly in high-technology products and a renewed attention to long-term needs through greater investment in research and development in the private sector. In addition, the United States should act to support American companies when foreign mercantilist practices demand a response in order to avoid harm.

A Renewed Emphasis upon Development

The burning problem of Third World debt must be urgently addressed. While a welcome first step, the Brady plan to reduce debt obligations must be pushed forward as far and as fast as possible. Expectations are high, especially in Latin America, and must not be disappointed. Twelve Latin American nations hold elections in the next eighteen months, and growth must be restored promptly to sustain democracy and stability. Mexico is the most pressing and important of these nations to the United States. Debt reduction must be accompanied by a flow of new resources and economic reforms in the debtor countries. The surplus nations, most notably Japan, must play a major role in financing debt relief, but the United States cannot be a free-rider. Given its own budget constraints, the United States should reallocate expenditures within its current aid budgets and act to expand more borrowing from international financial institutions by encouraging them to more fully utilize their guarantee authority. Reducing its own budget deficit would also lower interest rates, benefitting both ourselves and Third World debtors. It is imperative to reverse the flow of resources from South to North.

Easing the debt burden will not spur economic growth without new measures to expand trade opportunities, too. Preferential treatment for exports of the developing nations is no longer the central issue. The industrialized countries can make important concessions, such as liberalization of trade in textiles and sugar as well as abolishing all barriers to exports from the poorest nations. The developing countries, however, should now be prepared to join in agreement on issues such as international investment, intellectual property, and services and expose their economies to more competition through liberalization of trade barriers and restrictions. The developing nations should also play a greater role in the formation of international economic policy as well as accepting increasing responsibilities in the system, especially the newly industrializing nations.

It should be noted that regional needs now differ somewhat for these nations. South Asia is graduating from highly concessional terms to assistance from the World Bank, and thus the resources of the International Development Assistance (IDA) and other concessional lending should be increasingly directed to sub-Saharan Africa. The administration of the regional development banks and the specialized U.N. agencies should also be reformed to serve more effectively as bridges between the First and Third Worlds.

A New Economic Approach toward the Soviet Union and Eastern Europe

These nations should be more fully integrated into the international economic system to the extent that they are able and willing to accept responsibilities. We support increased contact between the Soviet Union and international economic institutions, to promote an exchange of information and discuss the rules and practices of the international economic system, though full membership is now premature. The Western democracies should seek greater economic openness and political pluralism in the nations of Eastern Europe and their expanded relations with multilateral economic institutions, recognizing the momentous possibilities that now exist there. The United States and its partners should not hesitate to differentiate between Eastern European countries in order to encourage the desired political evolution. The West should not negotiate specific new security arrangements with the Soviet Union regarding the future status of Eastern Europe, but it should make clear to the Soviets through the CSCE framework that it is not seeking to threaten Soviet security.

Reinforcing International Financial Institutions

The United States has not paid enough attention to multilateral institutions in the past. President Bush and leaders of other nations must take a more active role in the Bretton Woods institutions. For example, the Uruguay Round offers a major opportunity for fundamental reform of the GATT. The United States must also promptly and willingly pay its bills, ending a practice that has been embarrassing for this country. It is especially important that the roles of the participating nations reflect their economic contributions and standing. In particular, Japan is entitled to greater prominence. The United States must overcome its resistance to such changes and be willing to give up its veto power in the IMF and World Bank.

In all of these areas, American leadership is critical to success. While the United States is no longer dominant, it is still unique in its combination of economic strength, military power, technological prowess, and political vitality. At the same time, America must now learn to share the stage with other nations. The transition ahead will bring frequent frustrations, even acrimony, among the industrialized nations, but the United States should continue to welcome the emergence of other powers. They can and must accept some of the responsibilities as well as the costs of leadership.

Dean Acheson once wrote of the enormous excitement of being "present at the creation." Another such moment is at hand. If the industrialized democracies fail to seize the moment they risk serious global economic, political, and ecological crises within the decade. So taking advantage of the opportunity is not a choice but a major and urgent obligation. If, on the other hand, they do act together, and in cooperation with the developing nations, clearing away the imbalances of the global economy and building an open, dynamic world trading system, we could be on the verge of the most important—and most fulfilling—decade of this century, preparing a promising road for the twenty-first century.

To repeat, this is a watershed time. Failure to act would reflect a refusal to learn from history. The postwar era was built by men and women who insisted we learn from the panic, the Great Depression, and the Second World War. The world they built has served us well. The lesson of their political will, courage, and foresight is one we must now heed.

Participants
The Seventy-Sixth American Assembly

† THELMA J. ASKEY
Minority Trade Counsel
Committee on Ways and
 Means
U.S. House of
 Representatives
Washington, D.C.

† CLAUDE E. BARFIELD
Director, Science and
 Technology Policy Studies
American Enterprise
 Institute for Public Policy
 Research
Washington, D.C.

DOUGLAS J. BENNET, JR.
President
National Public Radio
Washington, D.C.

DOUG BEREUTER
Congressman from
 Nebraska
U.S. House of
 Representatives
Washington, D.C.

CHRISTINE A.
 BOGDANOWICZ-
 BINDERT
Senior Vice President
Shearson Lehman Hutton
 Inc.
New York and Frankfurt
 (Germany)

WILLIAM E. BROCK
President
The Brock Group
Washington, D.C.

PAT CHOATE
Vice President
Policy Analysis
TRW, Inc.
Arlington, Virginia

JAN V. DAUMAN
President
Intermatrix, Inc.
Westport, Connecticut

HANS W. DECKER
President
Siemens Corporation
New York, New York

GEZA FEKETEKUTY
Counselor to the U.S. Trade
 Representative
Office of the U.S. Trade
 Representative
Washington, D.C.

ROBERT H. FINCH
Attorney at Law
Fleming, Anderson,
 McClung & Finch
Pasadena, California

ROBERT J. FLEMING
Chairman
Robert Fleming
 International Research
 Inc.
Toronto, Ontario, Canada

STEPHEN J. FRIEDMAN
Executive Vice President
and General Counsel
The Equitable Financial
Companies
New York, New York

RICHARD N. GARDNER
Henry L. Moses Professor of
Law and International
Organization
School of Law
Columbia University
New York, New York

** DAVID R. GERGEN
Editor-at-Large
US News & World Report
Washington, D.C.

LINCOLN GORDON
Guest Scholar
Foreign Policy Studies
Program
The Brookings Institution
Washington, D.C.

JOHN A.M. GRANT
Executive Director
Corporate Strategy Staff
Ford Motor Company
Dearborn, Michigan

† MASAMICHI HANABUSA
Consul General of Japan
New York, New York

† MAHBUB UL HAQ
Senator
Pakistan Parliament
Islamabad, Pakistan

F. WILLIAM HAWLEY
Director of International
Government Relations
Citicorp
Washington, D.C.

ROBERT C. HELANDER
Jones Day Reavis & Pogue
New York, New York

FREDERICK HELDRING
Chairman
Global Interdependence
Center
Philadelphia, Pennsylvania

ROBERT D. HORMATS
Vice Chairman
Goldman Sachs International
New York, New York

† RICHARD HORNIK
National Economics
Correspondent
Time
Washington, D.C.

** KAREN ELLIOTT HOUSE
Vice President/International
Dow Jones & Co.
New York, New York

PIERRE JACQUET
Associate Director
Head of Economic Studies
French Institute of
International Relations
(IFRI)
Paris, France

* JAMES R. JONES
Partner
Dickstein, Shapiro & Morin
Washington, D.C.

PETER T. JONES
Adjunct Professor
School of Business
  Administration
University of California
Berkeley, California

PETER B. KENEN
Professor of Economics &
  Director of the
  International Finance
  Section
Department of Economics
Princeton University
Princeton, New Jersey

UWE KITZINGER
President
Templeton College
Oxford, England

** LOUIS KRAAR
Board of Editors
Fortune
New York, New York

GEOFFREY B. LAMB
Adviser
Strategic Planning and
  Review Department
The World Bank
Washington, D.C.

ROGER E. LEVIEN
Vice President
Strategy Office
Xerox Corporation
Stamford, Connecticut

PETER W. LUDLOW
Director
Centre for European Policy
  Studies
Brussels, Belgium

JESSICA TUCHMAN
  MATHEWS
Vice President
World Resources Institute
Washington, D.C.

ROBERT S. MCNAMARA
Washington, D.C.

† JOSEPH S. NYE, JR.
Director
Center for Science and
  International Affairs
John F. Kennedy School of
  Government
Harvard University
Cambridge, Massachusetts

BERNARD OSTRY
Chairman & Chief Executive
  Officer
TV Ontario
Toronto, Ontario, Canada

SYLVIA OSTRY
Senior Research Fellow
University of Toronto
Toronto, Ontario, Canada

VICTOR PALMIERI
Chairman
The Palmieri Company
New York, New York

JORGE F. PEREZ-LOPEZ
Director
Office of International
  Economic Affairs
U.S. Department of Labor
Washington, D.C.

GERALD A. REGAN
President
Hawthorne Developmental
  Services
Ottawa, Ontario, Canada

WILLIAM A. REINSCH
Chief Legislative Assistant
Office of Senator John Heinz
Washington, D.C.

WALT W. ROSTOW
Rex G. Baker, Jr. Professor of
  Political Economy
University of Texas
Austin, Texas

† WOLFGANG ROTH
Member of Parliament
Federal Republic of Germany

HERBERT SALZMAN
Partner
Bradford Associates
Princeton, New Jersey

HOWARD D. SAMUEL
President
Industrial Union Department
AFL-CIO
Washington, D.C.

ISABEL V. SAWHILL
Senior Fellow
The Urban Institute
Washington, D.C.

SUSAN C. SCHWAB
Assistant Secretary and
  Director
  General-Designate for U.S.
  and F.C.S.
U.S. Department of
  Commerce
Washington, D.C.

* JOHN W. SEWELL
President
Overseas Development
  Council
Washington, D.C.

MICHAEL B. SMITH
President
S.J.S. Advanced Strategies
Washington, D.C.

RICHARD H. SOLOMON
Assistant
  Secretary-Designate for
  East Asian and Pacific
  Affairs
U.S. Department of State
Washington, D.C.

STEPHEN STAMAS
President
New York Philharmonic
New York, New York

JOHN STREMLAU
Strategy Planning Division
The World Bank
Washington, D.C.

KAZUO TAKAHASHI
Program Director
Sasakawa Peace Foundation
Tokyo, Japan

CHARLES WOLF, JR.
Dean
The RAND Graduate School
The RAND Corporation
Santa Monica, California

** MARTIN WOLF
Chief Economics Leader
  Writer
Financial Times
London, England

JAMES D. WOLFENSOHN
President
James D. Wolfensohn, Inc.
New York, New York

* ALAN WM. WOLFF
Partner
Dewey, Ballantine, Bushby,
    Palmer & Wood
Washington, D.C.

TADASHI YAMAMOTO
President
The Japan Center for
    International Exchange
Tokyo, Japan

* Discussion Leader
** Rapporteur
† Panel Member

About The American Assembly

The American Assembly was established by Dwight D. Eisenhower at Columbia University in 1950. It holds nonpartisan meetings and publishes authoritative books to illuminate issues of United States policy.

An affiliate of Columbia, with offices on the Barnard College campus, the Assembly is a national educational institution incorporated in the state of New York.

The Assembly seeks to provide information, stimulate discussion, and evoke independent conclusions in matters of vital public interest.

American Assembly Sessions

At least two national programs are initiated each year. Authorities are retained to write background papers presenting essential data and defining the main issues in each subject.

A group of men and women representing a broad range of experience, competence, and American leadership meet for several days to discuss the Assembly topic and consider alternatives for national policy.

All Assemblies follow the same procedure. The background papers are sent to participants in advance of the Assembly. The Assembly meets in small groups for four or five lengthy periods. All groups use the same agenda. At the close of these informal sessions participants adopt in plenary session a final report of findings and recommendations.

Regional, state, and local Assemblies are held following the national session at Arden House. Assemblies have also been held in England, Switzerland, Malaysia, Canada, the Caribbean, South America, Central America, the Philippines, and Japan. Over 150 institutions have co-sponsored one or more Assemblies.

Arden House

Home of the American Assembly and scene of the national sessions is Arden House, which was given to Columbia University in 1950 by W. Averell Harriman. E. Roland Harriman joined his brother in contributing toward adaptation of the property for conference purposes. The buildings and surrounding land, known as the Harriman Campus of Columbia University, are 50 miles north of New York City.

Arden House is a distinguished conference center. It is self-supporting and operates throughout the year for use by organizations with educational objectives.

Index